Ultimate Nanny

Ultimate Nanny

HOW TO FIND, INTERVIEW, AND
MANAGE THE MOST IMPORTANT
PERSON YOU WILL EVER HIRE --
YOUR CHILD'S NANNY

● ● ●

Kristen J. Duca

The anecdotes included in this book are not necessarily based upon the experiences of individuals. Some stories in this book are composites of actual events. The names and identifying characteristics of some persons described in this book have been changed.

This book is written as a source of information only.

The publisher and the author make no representations or warranties with respect to the accuracy or completeness of the contents of this work and specifically disclaim all warranties, including, without limitation, warranties of fitness for a particular purpose. No warranty may be created or extended by sales or promotional materials. The advice and strategies contained herein may not be suitable for every situation. This work is sold with the understanding that the publisher and the author are not engaged in rendering legal, accounting, or other professional services. If professional assistance is required, the services of a competent professional person should be sought. Neither the publisher nor the author shall be liable for damages arising herefrom.

Some of the exercises and dietary suggestions contained in this work may not be appropriate for all individuals, and readers should consult with a physician before commencing any exercise or dietary program.

All efforts have been made to ensure the accuracy of the information contained in this book as of the date published. The author and the publisher expressly disclaim responsibility for any adverse effects arising from the use or application of the information contained herein.

ISBN-13: 9781530492046
ISBN-10: 1530492041
Library of Congress Control Number: 2016904442
CreateSpace Independent Publishing Platform
North Charleston, South Carolina

To Ken, Milla, and Arden for adding spice, laughter, chaos, and joy to my life through every inning.

Special acknowledgment and thanks to my parents, John and Joyce Barczyk, as well as my siblings—Matthew, Jonathan, and Amanda, and their families—for their undying enthusiasm, inspiration, and energy.

Table of Contents

Preface: How *Ultimate Nanny* Works for You · · · · · · · · · · · · · · · ·ix
Introduction: Exploring Your Childcare Needs · · · · · · · · · · · · · · · · · · ·xi

Chapter 1   Background: Check Closet and Set Course· · · · · · · · · · · · 1
Chapter 2   Hours, Travel, Compensation: Crafting the Deal· · · · · · 17
Chapter 3   Punctuality, Transportation, Vacations:
              Clear Expectations · 36
Chapter 4   Motivation, Desire, Character: Nanny Management · · · 42
Chapter 5   House Rules, Daily Routine, Chores, Grooming:
              Structuring the Job· 60
Chapter 6   Typical Day: Modeling Your Nanny's Day · · · · · · · · · · 100
Chapter 7   Safety and Pets: An Extra Level of Protection · · · · · · · 124
Chapter 8   Situational Questions: 360 Degrees of Insight · · · · · · · 136
Chapter 9   Final Question: Final Answer · · · · · · · · · · · · · · · · · · · 146

Appendix: Comprehensive List of Questions · · · · · · · · · · · · · · · · 149

How *Ultimate Nanny* Works for You

• • •

STARING DOWN AT YOUR NEW bundle of joy, you might think, "It is going to be impossible to find the perfect caring and responsible nanny to take care of this baby." It is not impossible. Yes, finding the ideal caretaker for your child requires a lot of time and hard work. However, if you put the effort into the search up front, you will be rewarded with the result.

The issue of childcare affects all families in every community regardless of socioeconomic background, religion, or race. Whether you need childcare because you are returning to work, craving some time to yourself, or spending some alone time with your significant other, you will have to evaluate several potential candidates.

It is never easy to leave your child in the care of someone else. But just how thorough your evaluation is will depend on your personality. Do not rush the nanny search. Finding the ideal person to take care of your little angel will take time and patience. You should be prepared and detailed in your search. You will want to conduct interviews (by phone, in person, or via webcam) with potential candidates in order to screen them through a series of questions. You need to ask prospective candidates the right questions in order to narrow down your list and eventually pick a suitable nanny for your family.

If possible, try to interview candidates in person so you can see their immediate reactions, facial expressions, and overall poise. These interviews do not have to be conducted in your home. You can always meet up for coffee/tea at a local diner or coffee shop or get together at another mutually convenient location such as a library or bookstore. Importantly, try to arrange an interview time that works for the nanny candidate as well as for you and your significant other. If it is impossible to coordinate schedules and you feel like you have a very strong nanny candidate who may work for your family, then have your significant other meet the candidate separately. Remember, selecting a nanny to care for your pride and joy is an important decision and one that requires the efforts of both parties. Would you hire an employee at your workplace without having him or her meet your boss or a coworker?

You may luck out and hire the first nanny you meet, or you might have to interview several candidates. Everyone has a different experience, but if you are dedicated to the nanny search, you will find the best candidate for your family. Always go with your gut, and trust your instincts.

This book will serve as a tool to guide you through the process of selecting a nanny or childcare provider. It will give you the foundation to develop your own list of questions and criteria. The book will also empower you with the methods you need to guide you in your quest for the ultimate nanny, as well as provide helpful tips for managing your nanny once you find her. Hopefully, the book will aid you in getting through a process that may not only be intimidating but also stressful. Please note that I am not a medical professional, attorney, employment counselor, childcare expert, accountant, or financial planner, so always consult the appropriate specialist or advisor for his or her expertise and advice.

Bottom line, it is imperative that you feel comfortable leaving your little one in someone else's care. If you are armed with tools to get you there, then you are one step closer to sleeping at night...or at least receiving an appropriate level of comfort. In the end, you need to know that you made the perfect decision for your little one. As long as you are confident that you approached the process with precision and prudence, you may even enjoy the flexibility that having a nanny gives you.

INTRODUCTION:

Exploring Your Childcare Needs

● ● ●

IF ASKED WHICH ANIMAL THEY would most want to be, most parents would likely say an octopus. Having the gift of four pairs of arms would be extremely beneficial in dealing with childcare. Unfortunately, we humans can only dream of having enough arms to tackle it all.

After childbirth, the reality soon sets in that for the first time in your adult life you may have to ask a stranger to come into your life to support you and your family with various childcare needs. Until you have a little one staring up at you, you may have never needed an extra hand in your home. But, now you do.

Hiring a caregiver to look after your child is your business and a very personal decision. Every family has its own dynamics and unique views on parenting. These differences among members of our society should be respected. So, if your mother-in-law exclaims, "How could you?" upon hearing you hired a nanny, feel free to tell her to buzz off. The same is true for the busybody you encounter in the grocery store or the annoying neighbor you run into in the elevator. Deciding whether to hire a nanny is sort of akin to deciding whether to breastfeed. To each her own. Feel secure and confident in your child-rearing decisions, and do not worry about the unsolicited advice or opinions of others.

The reasons you may need to hire an extra hand are vast and include the following:

- You have a job/career responsibilities.
- You do not have a supportive family network nearby.

- You want an extra hand so you can do errands (shopping, banking, going to doctor appointments).
- You take classes.
- You have a regular fitness regime that you wish to maintain.
- You want to spend time alone with your partner.
- You want to spend some one-on-one time separately with each of your children.
- You travel.
- You have a very busy social life (work, philanthropy, school events, business obligations).
- You have a child who needs extra assistance.
- You have multiple projects going on simultaneously (businesses, investments, real estate).
- You have responsibilities within your community.
- YOU JUST WANT A BREAK.

As trite and cliché as it sounds, it does take a village to raise a child, and either you have a village, or you need to build it through partnerships with others. You may have family members nearby, but are they capable caretakers who actually have time in their schedules to watch your child? Some parents have trusted housekeepers (including bilingual ones) who are terrific with children. They are willing to stay an extra hour here and there so the parents can run to an appointment or do an errand. However, other parents need consistent, reliable childcare on a weekly basis throughout the year and have to look outside their home for the solution.

As your child changes or your family dynamics change, your childcare needs will change. These childcare needs will constantly evolve as your child blossoms through the stages of life. It is important to realize that you are not pigeonholed into the first childcare situation you created at a specific point in time.

A situation that works for your newborn child will likely need to be scrapped, tweaked, or revised as your child starts school. Additionally, a childcare provider who is great with babies who need many diaper changes and tummy-time stimulation may not be ideal for school-aged children who need help with reading and mathematics.

As you look at your childcare provider cradling your baby in her arms and whispering sweet lullabies, you may have dreams of inviting her one day to your grown child's wedding. Even though some childcare relationships do withstand the test of time, many do not. Although it is difficult, you may have to relinquish control a bit. You may have to realize that expecting the unexpected and having the ability to be nimble is crucial to formulating the right childcare situation at any given point in time.

There are myriad childcare options for your family to ponder together. The ideal situation for your family may be dramatically different from that of a neighbor, a dear friend, or a sibling. Realizing this may help you deal with unsolicited advice that will inevitably smack you in the face. The groundwork toward building the ideal childcare situation depends on the following factors:

1. **Your child/children:** ages, developmental stages, and needs
2. **You:** work/social schedules, flexibility in the hours you need childcare help
3. **Your family:** Are you hiring solely for childcare? Do you also need assistance with housekeeping, cooking, cleaning, pet care, and errands?
4. **Layers of help:** Are there suitable, willing family members or friends nearby who can help you in a pinch?

Delving into each of these factors further will help you assess what exactly you are hiring for presently. Formulating a clear description of your childcare needs now will save you loads of future frustration. You can zero in on exactly what type of situation you need to make sure your household runs smoothly and happily.

Thinking about your personal childcare needs starts with you. The ideal or "perfect" childcare situation depends on you and how specific you are in recognizing and expressing your needs, as well as on how your family spends its time. It is important that before you start your childcare search you set aside time to sit down and ponder the following:

- What are the various types of childcare options?
- Which type of childcare situation do you feel is right for you today? Do you want someone who solely spends time with your kids? Do you also need help with other household duties such as cooking, cleaning, pet care, homework, errands, and so on?
- What questions do you have for the prospective childcare provider? How will you deal with your childcare provider's vacation/sick/personal days? It is important to set expectations early.
- How many hours/days a week do you need childcare assistance? Do you travel? Do you have unusual hours?
- How do you want to incorporate your childcare provider into your family? Will your childcare provider eat with your family? Will you provide meals? Does your childcare provider have any allergies to pets or food and so on?
- Can one person handle it all, or do you need a few people?

Keep in mind that it is OK to ask for help with your child. But be aware of what assistance you are asking for, and make sure it is reasonable. To put it bluntly, if you are not willing or able to do it all, then your childcare provider should not be expected to either.

Childcare providers are not superheroes. They are humans who have strengths, weaknesses, and feelings, just like you. As a rule of thumb, it is generally never a good idea to ask your childcare provider to do tasks that you cannot handle yourself. Be reasonable and fair with your requirements of your childcare provider. It is sort of like going into a dressing room with a size zero nonmaternity dress while you are nine months pregnant...chances are it may not fit. And one size also does not fit all.

A multitude of childcare possibilities exist for you to consider, and of course there are pluses and minuses to each of them. Just remember that you are in the driver's seat and can choose the path that best fits your family's needs. Some examples are as follows:

Day care: *Day care* could be a nice option for parents who work a set schedule of hours that are aligned to those of the day-care facility. Some employers even have full-time day-care facilities on their premises, while others may have backup/emergency day-care options for their employees to use as long as they have up-to-date applications on file.

Many parents will have to look outside of their work situation for a day-care facility for their child that is convenient to either their place of employment or their home. Day care is usually less expensive compared to a one-on-one childcare situation due to economies of scale. The ratio of children to day-care workers is higher compared to other options. However, if you tend to have unpredictable hours at your job (last-minute meetings, travel, and so on) that cause you to stay late or arrive early on occasion, you may have to eliminate day care as a viable option for your family. Parents who put their children in day care must adhere to the center's rules and health standards—meaning if your child is ill, he or she may not be welcome at the day-care center that day. Thus, the family must have a backup plan in such situations.

Also, your family must be on board with putting your child in a group situation where he or she may or may not get constant one-on-one attention, stimulation, or interaction. Some day-care facilities offer more limited educational curriculums. However, other day-care centers provide solid learning resources as well as educational programs and creative activities that will aid in the developmental growth of your child. Certain day-care programs have structures similar to preschool programs, complete with early literacy and math instruction as well as music and art periods. Children in these types of day-care settings learn social skills at an early age in a nurturing setting that may be a wonderful foundation for future schooling—not to mention discovering the joy of learning as toddlers.

Mother's helper: If you have a flexible schedule and only need someone to watch your child periodically for a few hours at a time while you are at home, you may want to consider hiring a mother's helper. A *mother's helper* is someone who comes over to spend time with your child (playing games, reading, and so on). Therefore, she gives you a well-deserved break or time to focus on other things (cleaning, paying bills, cooking, organizing, and so on).

Typically, a mother's helper is a high-school-aged student who enjoys working with children and wants to earn a little money to supplement her weekly allowance. Mother's helpers are often found through word-of-mouth communications with friends, neighbors, coworkers, or religious organizations or through community postings online or off-line.

Parents usually structure the time a mother's helper spends with their child by suggesting or putting out a few different play-based activities or projects for them to work on together. The mother's helper should also feel welcome to have the child partake in fun projects she enjoyed as a child, such as dressing up and putting on a show or making snowflakes out of paper. For many students, being a mother's helper is their first job. Some mother's helpers end up parlaying their experience gained with children into counseling jobs at camps or babysitting jobs as they get older.

Part-time babysitter: A *part-time babysitter* may be a college student who would like to earn a little spending money while adding experience with children to her résumé. Or, she may be an adult who loves children and wants to supplement her income watching them on a part-time basis. Many times, college or graduate students have flexible schedules that enable them to be "on call" for families when babysitting requests arise. Adult babysitters may be family members or friends who just enjoy children and find entertaining them to be a nice source of extra revenue.

It is important to note that all part-time babysitters should be compensated fairly at an agreed-upon rate. If a family member does not want to accept money, you may find another way to express your gratitude—possibly with gift cards, event tickets, restaurant certificates, and so on. This way, if you have any constructive criticism or advice to give family members who babysit, they will be more receptive. They will realize you consider their time spent with your child to be a job, not a hobby.

Parents need to ensure that student-aged babysitters have the maturity to handle watching their child. The babysitter should spend time wisely with the child as opposed to plopping him or her in front of a television, computer, video game, or other electronic device—not to mention raiding your refrigerator as well. And, make it perfectly clear that the friends of babysitters are not permitted to visit your home while they are on duty caring for your child.

If the babysitter you hire has a pleasant disposition and properly engages your child with fun activities, your child may not mind if you step out once in a while.

Nanny share: There are two common *nanny share* arrangements. In the first type, two families share the hours a nanny is available and willing to work each week, thus creating a consistent schedule. The shared nanny may work for one family on Monday, Wednesday, and Friday and the other family on Tuesdays and Thursdays. The nanny shifts between households depending on the day, and each family pays for its portion of her time worked. The two families do not interact in regard to the nanny unless they need to swap a day or discuss vacation schedules.

The second type of a nanny share involves two families using one nanny at the same time. Usually, the nanny spends one week at one family's house caring for both families' children and then spends the following week at the other family's house. The parents are responsible for dropping off their child every other week. If one child falls ill, then the nanny usually goes to the house with the healthy child (or children) until the other child is better, thus not exposing the other children to sickness. This type of childcare arrangement may present a more affordable option compared to each family hiring its own nanny. However, the children of both families must get along in order for it to work out. With nanny shares, remember that each state has its own rules and regulations about what constitutes day care in a personal residence. So, you must be aware of the number of children that will be involved in the nanny share, especially when siblings come into the mix.

Nanny: A *nanny* is an adult who works for your family in your residence on a weekly basis with a set schedule. A nanny's schedule may allow for vacation and sick and personal days. Nannies may assist working parents or may be an extra hand for parents with busy schedules or those who need breaks during the day.

The tasks of a nanny are usually routine and geared toward supporting your child throughout the day. The nanny's responsibilities may include assisting your child with dressing, feeding, brushing teeth, grooming, bathing, transporting to classes/lessons/playdates/school/parties/social functions, entertaining, playing, reading, and homework.

For working parents, nannies may also take the child to prearranged doctor, dentist, or therapy appointments (where the parents may meet them). Some families request that their nannies accompany them to weekend houses or on vacations throughout the year and pay for all expenses incurred.

Nannies may be asked to assist with the child's laundry, meal preparation, and room organization. Nannies can be found through leads from friends, community newsletters or blogs, agencies, or websites. Nanny compensation should always be discussed in advance of the job's start date.

Live-in nanny: A *live-in nanny* does just that—she lives with your family. Some of these nannies go home on weekends, while others stay with your family full-time. In a live-in situation, parents set up a proper and comfortable bedroom and bathroom for their nanny as well as provide meals for her. Live-in nannies are ideal for parents who have atypical or unusual working hours (nights/weekends) or busy travel schedules. These nannies ideally do become an extension of the child's family and should be treated as such.

Au pair: With an *au pair* relationship, the family commits to a cultural exchange for a defined amount of time. It is facilitated through registered agencies that thoroughly prescreen potential childcare candidates from various countries.

Au pairs are often college-aged students who strongly desire to live abroad with a family, and they take care of a family's child in exchange for room, board, and a stipend. The duration of their work relationship with a family is limited, as they have to go back to their home country after a certain amount of time has passed. However, they do become an integrated family member for the time spent in their family's home.

Au pairs tend to be less expensive than most live-in nannies, given their age and experience level. However, many parents feel their energy level, excitement, and cultural teachings can enrich their child's life. Some au pairs help teach children another language inside the home. Agencies do limit the hours an au pair can work on a weekly basis. Remember that whether or not the au pair is "on the clock" caring for your child, she still lives under your roof. Au pairs should be looked after and treated with kindness and respect.

As every community is very different, there is no one source to turn to in the search for a childcare provider. Moreover, you will most likely have to conduct your thorough childcare provider search via several sources that may include the following:

- word of mouth (friends/relatives)
- referrals from other parents or childcare providers
- religious organizations or religious leaders (newsletters, weeklies)
- college bulletin boards, college newspapers, or online college classifieds or job postings
- local schools
- physicians' offices
- birthing centers
- nurses and receptionists
- health-care workers
- prenatal exercise studios
- agencies (be prepared to pay appropriate fees)
- online childcare-solutions
- community centers
- local newspapers or publications (hard copy or online)
- local women's clubs with message boards or networking
- playgrounds or parks

No matter where you turn in your childcare-provider search, always remember to conduct a thorough interview and check references. Suggest she start working with your family on a trial basis so you can ensure you find the right fit for your family.

Although the text of this book uses language more appropriate to childcare situations involving a nanny, the content can be used broadly across all areas of childcare. Also, for ease of reading, the text usually uses the feminine pronouns *she* and *her* to refer to a nanny. Just remember, the more prepared parents are when meeting a potential childcare provider, the more at ease they will be with their hiring decision. A happy child makes for a happy parent.

CHAPTER 1

Background: Check Closet and Set Course

● ● ●

WHILE YOU MAY NOT FIND any skeletons in the closet, you may discover some potential incompatibility problems, habits, or personality traits that make a candidate less than ideal. If you notice these red flags during the interview process, it will save you lots of time and heartache later. A carefully crafted initial interview is essential to taking the first big step in the right direction.

Question: How long have you been a nanny?
Follow-up: Where do you see yourself in the future?

It is important for you to find out how long the nanny candidate has been a nanny. Ask her why and when she decided to become a nanny. Find out what made her decide to work in other people's homes as a nanny as opposed to working in a day-care facility or a nursery school. Watch her expressions as she discusses children.

- Does she look you in the eye when answering questions?
- Is she excited when she talks about children?
- Does she seem to have a real passion for childcare?
- Does she seem genuine?
- Does she seem to have ulterior motives?
- Does she love working as a nanny?

Be careful if the nanny candidate tells you she works as a nanny because she views it as an easy job that pays well. If she claims she is a nanny because many of her friends are nannies, then examine whether childcare is really her true passion. If she admits that she had difficulties keeping other jobs in the past, then ask her to expand upon her comments so you can gain a better understanding of her previous employment situations.

One mother was extremely disappointed during the initial interview. The nanny candidate admitted she had started as a cleaning person or housekeeper. She switched careers to become a nanny because it paid more. The mother did not feel the nanny candidate really had her heart in the childcare profession.

You should ask the nanny candidate where she envisions herself to be longer term with regard to her professional ambitions.

- Does she still want to be in the childcare profession?
- Does she desire employment in another field of work?
- Does she seem to have reasonable goals for her future?

One father mentioned how thrilled he was as the nanny candidate beamed when talking about caring for children. She was extremely enthusiastic about working with children and teaching them new things. She had even brought along pictures of the children she had cared for in the past. She explained that she still kept in touch with many of her previous families. When she could, she hopped on the train and commuted to visit a few families that had moved outside the immediate area. Her long-term goal was to save up enough money to start her own neighborhood dance school for children.

Question: How many children have you taken care of at once in one family?
Follow-up: How many children would you ideally like to care for at once?

It is not easy to look into the proverbial crystal ball and predict your family's childcare needs for years to come. Do keep in mind that your family's needs as well as size may change with time. Obviously, you cannot plan for everything (hello—TWINS), but if you are considering getting pregnant or adopting, thus adding another child (or children) to the mix, you may want to hire a nanny who is able and willing to handle your expanding family unit. What you need in terms of childcare today may not be what you will need in the future. However, taking time to reflect now may save you the time and effort of conducting interviews all over again later.

One newly pregnant mother (with baby number two) was happily surprised to find out that her nanny candidate ideally wanted to care for two children at once. As the parent of one child already, she was surprised that the nanny wanted the additional responsibility of caring for another child.

When the mother questioned why she thought taking care of two children was the perfect arrangement, the nanny replied that she loved to be busy and challenged. She expanded her thoughts by explaining that each child had his or her own distinct personality. She believed that it was very interesting to watch two children from the same home develop into completely separate individuals. She also said that depending on their ages, you may have to do a lot of juggling with activities. The nanny thought it was nice to have days filled with following two different schedules. She said she always looked forward to taking the children to their various activities or classes.

Although the mother was not yet ready to announce her second pregnancy to anybody she knew, she had found the perfect fit for her family. The nanny was hired.

Some nannies may have their own children or grandchildren. Other nannies may have worked for large families. These nannies may or may not be intimidated by the thought of caring for multiple children across many age groups.

Many nannies are more comfortable with a one-on-one childcare situation. These nannies desire employment by a family with only one child. In the initial interview, ask the nanny candidate how many children she would ideally like to care for at once. You don't want to hire a nanny who is uncomfortable with the size of your family.

Question: How long-term of a job are you looking for right now?
Follow-up: Will you try to give us advance notice if you need to leave the job with our family?

Depending on your family's situation, you may be required to hire a nanny on either a short- or long-term basis. You will want to communicate the expected duration of the job to your nanny candidates. As you know, hiring a nanny can often be a long and tedious process. So if you desire longevity in your nanny's employment with your family, make that clear in the first discussion. Some children—not to mention some parents—crave stability with their childcare providers, while others are perfectly comfortable with adding fresh energy to the household mix with a new nanny.

You will discover that some nanny candidates do not want to stay with one family for too long, while others prefer long-term working relationships with families they adore. You should find out the nanny candidate's expectations in terms of employment with your family up front.

One mother interviewed a candidate who had been a nanny for over fifteen years and had worked with only two families during that period. The nanny candidate desired employment with a family that would provide her longevity in her career. She admitted that she preferred to start a new job that required caring for an infant so that she could watch the child grow and develop in the upcoming years. She also desired a situation where she was not only the caregiver but also an extended family member. The mother was quite touched with the nanny's honesty and offered her a job caring for her newborn.

If the nanny candidate is enrolled in classes, be aware that her class schedule may change throughout the year. For example, you may be able to get her full days on Mondays and Wednesdays in the fall semester, but when the winter semester begins, her class schedule may be filled on those days. Additionally, her course work may change depending on her studies.

Even though the nanny candidate has plenty of free time to watch your child in the fall semester, she may not be able to squeeze the same amount of childcare hours into the winter semester. Make sure you are aware of the nanny candidate's current and future availability up front. Also, if a nanny signals to you that she travels a lot, she may not be able to watch your child on a consistent basis; this may affect your family's balance.

Circumstances do change, so you should be prepared to do another nanny search in the event that your nanny's employment with your family must end.

Question: Can I please have a list of names and phone numbers in order to check your references?
Follow-up: Why did each of your previous jobs end?

Encourage your nanny candidate to bring a résumé and list of references to the first interview. If the nanny candidate does not have a formal résumé (many do not), make sure you ask her for references from the last three (or more) families she worked for as a nanny. Ask the nanny candidate for specifics such as names, phone numbers, durations of jobs, and why the jobs ended. If the nanny candidate hesitates, then you may want to delve into the reasons she is not forthcoming about references.

If you are considering the candidate, then your next step will be to call these references and ask them some questions that you have prepared. You will find that many families are very open when it comes to the delicate subject of childcare. Some references may even offer to meet you face-to-face to answer any questions you have about the nanny.

It is important that you do not interrupt the references when they are speaking. By allowing them to talk freely, you may learn more than you thought you would. If something they say is unclear, then ask for clarification. If something they say is unsettling to you, then make sure to ask the other references similar questions about the nanny to find out if they give you the same response.

You may consider asking the family's references the following questions:

- How many children did the nanny watch?
- What were the ages of the children the nanny cared for (when the job began and ended)?
- How many hours and what hours did the nanny work?
- Was the nanny punctual?
- Describe the nanny's personality or general mood.
- What was the nanny's daily routine with the child (children)?
- What are some of the nanny's positive characteristics or traits?

- What are some of the nanny's negative characteristics or traits?
- What was the duration of employment?
- Why did the job end?
- Is there anything you should know about the nanny (positive or negative) that was not asked?
- Would you rehire the nanny?
- Would you recommend the nanny for employment?

The last question is very important because you will get an idea of who ended the relationship—the nanny or the family. Feel free to delve into the circumstances that led to the change. Some nannies enjoy change and do not intend to stay with the same family for long durations. Or, perhaps the family moved to another location, and it was no longer convenient for the nanny to commute. Maybe the children got older and their childcare needs changed.

Question: Have you ever been convicted of a crime?
Follow-up: Would you agree to submit to a background check?

Family safety is important to everyone. It is quite easy and inexpensive to find a professional company to conduct a background check on your nanny candidate if that is important to you. If you like a nanny candidate and are seriously considering her for the job, you should be forthcoming that you would like her to sign a release form so you can conduct a preemployment search on her before making a hiring decision. If she will be transporting your child by automobile, you may want to consider checking her driving record. If you do wish to go forward with conducting a background check on the nanny candidate, you may want to seek legal advice to make sure that proper procedures are followed.

Researching the nanny candidate's background on your own may also provide you with information as to her honesty, character, and maturity. It is not a bad idea to go on the Internet and search your nanny candidate's name to see what comes up online. Surfing the Internet and perusing social media pages do not take a lot of time and may shed light on another side to your potential caregiver.

Some parents have been shocked to find suggestive or inappropriate pictures and quotes from nanny candidates on the Internet. On the other hand, other parents have discovered positive aspects to their nanny candidate when searching online. One parent was happy to find out that her nanny candidate had cooking talents after she saw pictures online of cakes she had made and decorated. Another parent was excited to discover how many different organizations her nanny was involved in over the years. The nanny had a deep interest in supporting the arts as well as wildlife groups.

Question: Would you agree to a trial period before we make a decision for full-time employment?

Follow-up: Are you willing to work the same schedule during your trial period as you would if we brought you on full time? You would be compensated accordingly.

A trial period of a few days, a few weeks, or even a month is a good way to find out if your nanny's personality and style fit well with your family's. You could start by having the nanny "shadow" your daily routine so she learns how you do certain things for the child and where specific items are stored. Once you are confident that the nanny knows your child's schedule, you should leave the house for various amounts of time. See how she communicates with you in your absence:

- Does she answer her phone in a timely manner?
- Does she text you updates or questions?
- Is she comfortable contacting you?
- Does she write down or e-mail you any questions she has?

Additionally, you should pay attention to your child's mood when you return. Initially, you may hear your child cry as he or she experiences separation anxiety. If you are concerned, ask the nanny how long the crying lasted or what she did to soothe the child. You may even want to stand quietly outside your door and listen intensely to how the nanny interacts with your child.

One mother was completely turned off by the negativity the nanny projected during the trial period. When the mother cooked elaborate meals, the nanny told her it would be impossible for her to continue cooking like that when the child grew and needed more attention. The mother responded by telling her that cooking was relaxing for her and hiring a nanny was a treat that would free up some time for her to create and freeze dishes for the upcoming weeks. The nanny continued to debate the issue with her. Ultimately, the mother did not hire that nanny. She concluded that the constant arguments were inappropriate and that ultimately the child might suffer from hearing the disputes.

Another mother was shocked when the nanny brought her baby a balloon and beaded necklace as a gift during the trial period. The mother explained that both items were choking hazards to her child. She made it clear that she did not want her child exposed to such potential hazards again.

Of course, plenty of parents have found upside surprises during this trial period. For instance, one nanny came with her own origami kit and showed the children how to create flowers and animals by folding colorful paper. Another nanny taught the children to play a new board game. She also kindly encouraged them to tidy the playroom upon conclusion of the game.

During the trial period, watch how the nanny deals with the mundane childcare tasks at hand. For example, if the nanny is changing your child's dirty diaper, does she hold her nose and shake her head in disgust, or does she happily change the diaper as though she's done it several times before? If she is playing cards with your child, does she make friendly, upbeat conversation to engage and encourage the child, or does she play in silence? Ultimately, you want your child to develop confidence. So if your nanny has a positive attitude throughout your child's day and tries to continuously engage him or her, then the child is one step closer to growing up to become a strong, well-adjusted individual.

Question: Would you be willing to review a nanny agreement with us?
Follow-up: Would you sign the agreement once you review it? (Keep one copy and return the other copy to us.)

It is a good idea to create a "nanny agreement" or a "nanny responsibility code" before hiring a nanny. First, it will force you to come to an agreement on exactly what you expect of her and what she can expect of you. Second, the agreement will give you a chance to put everything in one place so there is no ambiguity, thus lessening future debates or arguments about her role. Third, by reviewing the document or agreement together as a team, you will begin your relationship with your nanny on a solid foundation.

It is important that you allow her to communicate to you any questions, concerns, or comments she has regarding the agreement and make alterations if necessary. Also, make it clear you understand that certain unforeseen events may come up. You will respect her, treat her fairly, and ask that she does the same. For instance, if she is normally on time and happens to be late for work one day due to the subways not running on time or her car breaking down let her know that her safety is of utmost importance and that she will not be penalized. Additionally, it is always best to check with a lawyer or a financial or medical professional if you have any questions about anything in your proposed nanny agreement.

Some items or terms you may want to include on your nanny agreement are as follows:

- the date
- your name, address, and phone number(s)
- your child's name and date of birth
- the nanny's name, address, and phone number(s)
- hours and days of week she is expected to work
- pay as well as overtime pay if applicable and any other benefits
- basis of compensation
- payday

- paid time off, vacation days, personal days, and so on
- performance reviews, raises, bonuses
- sick-day policy
- specific schedule, including exact start and end times expected each day
- specific responsibilities or duties
- house rules for your family
- policies for your family on discipline, electronics, eating, sleeping, and so on
- transportation requirements
- emergency contact details for the child
- emergency contact details for the nanny
- confidentiality agreement so the nanny understands family information is private
- termination or discipline agreement for the nanny
- reimbursement for transportation, meals, childcare courses, cell phones, and other allowances
- your signature/date and the nanny's signature/date

Finally, if something in the agreement changes during the duration of your nanny's employment with you, then you should edit or update the details on paper. Make two copies of the new agreement so each of you can initial or sign the amended document.

Question: Would you like to take a tour of our home?
Follow-up: Do you think our setup is appropriate for our child's needs?

Treat the nanny candidate with the same respect you would a guest entering your home. If you have a good feeling about the nanny candidate after you ask her most of your prepared interview questions, then offer to give her a brief tour of your home. You do not have to go through every room. However, you will want to show her the main rooms that your child will frequent. Show her where your first-aid kits and fire extinguishers are kept. Reiterate that safety for your child and everyone in your home is top priority.

While you are showing her your residence, ask her if she has any feedback regarding how you have set up your home for your child. Asking the nanny candidate to review your living arrangement gives her the power to offer her advice or opinion. She may point out potential hazards to your child and suggest you add more childproofing devices. Perhaps she will make a few suggestions to increase your efficiency or use of space. Maybe she has some advice based on her past work experiences that would make your home better for your child's growth. Or she may think everything looks great and compliment you on your organization.

Some parents lock up or hide items that they believe are too precious to be left out in the open. If you have valuable items, you may want to consider storing them out of plain sight.

If you have a computer, let her know your house rules on the use of technology. If you allow her to use your computer with or without your child present, you may want to specify times she is allowed to use it. For example, you may not have a problem if she goes online while your child is napping to look up schedules relating to local events for children or to download recipes. However, you may not want her spending too much time using your computer or her phone to surf the Internet while your child is awake.

Even though you may have to establish a lot of rules up front, it is better to be safe. Additionally, rule establishment may result in the avoidance of the destruction of expensive items. One father who collected antique wooden furniture told his nanny that all were welcome to use the antique tables for eating as long as tablecloths and coasters were put down prior to all meals. He made sure to instruct the nanny to keep all of the child's art supplies (crayons, markers, paint, and pens) away from the antique furniture.

If you have any precious artwork, antique furniture, or other valuable items, point them out to the nanny candidate during the tour of your home. Tell her that it is her responsibility to keep your child away from any priceless or important items. However, remember that your child is your most valuable asset and that even though he or she may be told to be careful numerous times, accidents do happen, whether you are present or not. The image of my childhood friend breaking his mother's antique vase with an "accidental" football toss comes to mind. At the end of the day, if you are so worried about an object, then keep it locked up somewhere safe.

CHAPTER 2

Hours, Travel, Compensation: Crafting the Deal

● ● ●

No FANCY TRICKS OR TECHNIQUES needed. The overarching principle here is to be fair and open. Both sides must clearly understand the hours, travel requirements, and compensation details for the relationship to work. The questions that follow will help ensure that your family and nanny are on the same page about these important issues.

Question: Would you be willing to share a full-time schedule with our family and our friend's family?

Follow-up: Could each family give you set days and hours?

Increasingly, people with children are working flexible schedules in order to strive for a desirable work/life/family balance. With work schedules that allow for flexible hours, parents may neither need nor want a nanny on a full-time basis.

However, many nannies still desire a full-time schedule along with the appropriate compensation to match. In an attempt to satisfy the nanny's needs, some parents decide to hire the nanny on a full-time basis even though they do not necessarily need a nanny for so many hours. The parents use the additional hours that the nanny is in their home looking after their child while they are not at work to run errands, exercise, prepare meals, engage in housekeeping, meet up with friends, shop for household goods, and so on.

If your budget allows you the luxury of employing a nanny for additional time to give you a chance to take care of personal errands, relations, or issues, then by all means—do it. If you do not have the financial means to employ a nanny for extra hours or if you want to spend the time when you are not at work alone with your child, then consider a nanny-share arrangement. If you have a friend who desires a similar childcare situation, you can jointly evaluate whether both families' childcare hours provide the nanny with enough hours and income to satisfy her needs. Obviously, you will have a problem if the hours both you and your friend desire overlap.

If you do not have a friend who also desires a nanny share, then you may need to do a little bit of researching and networking to find someone you could work with in a nanny-share situation. Have an idea of what hours and days you need the nanny to work for your family before you start your search.

One mother worked in an office on Tuesdays and Thursdays and needed to fill the nanny's schedule for Mondays, Wednesdays, and Fridays.

She sent out a blast e-mail to several friends, colleagues, and family members, and through her efforts, she was able to find someone who worked on a freelance basis and needed a nanny for her child three days a week. Because her former nanny had moved out of town, she not only needed to find a nanny but also a family to share the nanny with each week. It was a wonderful situation for everyone. The nanny was quite happy, as both families also offered her additional hours and compensation for staying late or working on occasional weekends.

Question: Would you be willing to work for us even though we also employ another nanny?

Follow-up: Do you have any hesitations about our "rotating nanny" arrangement?

Some families do not like the idea of hiring one nanny exclusively for the entire week. They do not want the nanny to get bored or overtired. As a result, they hire a few nannies who desire part-time or flexible work schedules with the hopes that each nanny will show up to work fresh and energized. Additionally, they believe that their child may learn more by getting various perspectives and experiencing different activities.

One mother who hired rotating nannies for her toddler raved about how each nanny brought something different to the childcare situation. One nanny engaged the toddler in a multitude of art and cooking projects in the mornings. Another nanny took the toddler to museums and playgrounds in the afternoons. And, both nannies spoke Spanish to the toddler. The mother also appreciated the spirit each of the nannies brought to the home and to the child. She admitted that she, too, constantly learned something new from each of the nannies. As a result, she believed she would be a better mother to her child with this knowledge and insight.

It is important to make sure the nanny candidate is receptive to a rotating-nanny situation. While some nannies welcome a flexible work schedule, others prefer a more traditional workweek. You do not want the nanny to feel like you do not think she is capable of taking care of your child on a full-time basis. You may need to explain to her your philosophy on rotating-nanny arrangements. Moreover, you do not want to get into a situation where the nanny feels jealousy or resentment toward you, your family, the other nannies, or your child.

Additionally, if you employ multiple nannies, then remember that organization is of utmost importance. You will want to clearly communicate the exact hours and days each nanny will work each week. Whether you create a master calendar or a detailed spreadsheet of hours that you need coverage, you will want to make sure the nannies know exactly when they will take care of your child. This will prevent any mistakes such as both nannies showing up for work at the same time. Also, take into consideration the vacation days and holidays that affect your nannies as well as your family. If you work together as a team, the arrangement should be positive and beneficial to all involved.

Question: Would you be able to work nontraditional hours?
Follow-up: How many nontraditional hours per week can you work?

It is hard to give a precise definition of "traditional hours" in a workweek. Many parents do not work from nine o'clock in the morning until five in the evening. While some parents need a few more hours on the earlier and later side, others need a whole different schedule. Be up front about the hours you expect your nanny to work on a weekly basis. Do not be afraid of scaring candidates or driving them away. You need to establish honest dialogue from the start, or else you may be disappointed when you find out that the nanny cannot change her schedule to fit yours.

You may be surprised to discover that some nannies are quite happy to work nontraditional hours. They can spend their off-work hours with their own families, further their education, or work in another capacity.

If you expect your nanny to work nontraditional hours you should think about the following:

- Do the nontraditional hours affect her ability to commute to your home? (Consider bus schedules and train schedules.)
- How many hours total do you need the nanny each week? Will you need her to work overtime? (If yes, then perhaps adjust her pay accordingly.)
- What is your backup plan if the nanny gets sick or cannot come to work for some reason?
- Are you expecting her to sleep over in your home? (If so, then you must provide her proper accommodations.)
- Will your hours "rotate" day to day, week to week, or month to month? (Detail your schedule up front.)
- Will you let her watch your child (children) out of her home?
- Do you expect your nanny to be "on call" and extremely responsive to your needs or requests as well as completely flexible with your schedule?

Once again, organization is the key ingredient in staffing a nanny with a nontraditional workweek. You will want to focus on hiring someone who is very dependable yet flexible, and you may have to pay more for such an arrangement.

Question: Are you flexible to work additional hours outside our normal schedule?
Follow-up: How late can you stay at night?

Whether your job needs you to stay late or you just want to have a nice date night with your partner, you may need a nanny that will give your family additional hours. If you require your nanny to work extra hours, then compensate her accordingly and appropriately, as required.

As a nice bonus for the favor, you may want to consider these options:

- giving her money for meals or having meals prepared or available for her
- paying for her cab fare home or providing her transportation home (such as a car service)
- presenting her with extra money or gifts for the special favor

Many nannies appreciate the extra income that is associated with additional hours. One mother was thrilled when her nanny asked for additional hours around the winter holidays so she could have more money for holiday shopping. The mother was able to attend both work- and non-work-related holiday parties, while the nanny was happy to put in extra hours. It was a win-win situation.

Just make sure you are not overworking your nanny because you do not want her to be burned out from taking care of your children. Always do a sanity check when you map out your week and be cognizant that your nanny needs to relax and sleep, too. For instance, if you come home one evening at twelve midnight, it may be difficult for the nanny to commute home, go to sleep, wake up, and then commute back to your home for a six o'clock start to the workday.

Be fair and rational in your expectations, and always ask her if the additional hours are OK with her rather than assume that she is fine with the workload. If you find that you do need your nanny to work a lot of additional hours in a certain week, then think about giving her something special for her efforts. Always keep in mind that you are tired if you don't get enough sleep and that your nanny is no different. At the end of the day, you want the person taking care of your child to be well rested, energetic, and happy.

Question: Would you be willing to stay overnight at our home when needed?

Follow-up: Is there anything special we can do to make your overnight stay with us more comfortable?

Whether you work the late shift, travel frequently, or desire an evening alone with your partner away from home, you may need overnight childcare services—as long as you have the appropriate space in your home. If you believe that overnight childcare assistance will be necessary, ask the nanny candidate up front if she is comfortable staying in your home alone with your child overnight. If she agrees to stay overnight, make sure you discuss her expected compensation before your excursion and pay her as appropriate.

You may want to consider the following questions:

- Was her overnight work in addition to the regular childcare hours she works for you?
- Did you adjust her regular childcare hours for her overnight work?
- Will you provide additional meals for her, such as dinner, breakfast, and various snacks?
- Is she familiar with your child's nighttime routine? If she is not, then give her a schedule and any additional information she may need. Take into consideration bathing, additional feedings, bedtime stories, and so on.
- Is she comfortable in your home? Remember, your big-city-living nanny may not be comfortable sleeping in your home, which is in the middle of the woods and lacks curtains.

Make sure your home is clean and organized if your nanny is sleeping overnight. Unless you have a prearrangement regarding cleaning as a requirement of your nanny's duties, do not expect to leave her with a messy home that needs to be cleaned while you are away.

Also, make sure the room she is sleeping in and the bathroom she is using have appropriate linens, clean towels, and other necessities. Travel bottles of shampoo, conditioner, shower gel, and lotion are always nice to put out for your nanny. Ask her in advance for a list of healthy foods and beverages that she would like to see in your home, and make sure you stock up before she arrives.

Question: Would you like to travel with us?
Follow-up: Will you pack for our child?

Whether you have to travel for work or pleasure, ask the nanny in advance if she is available and willing to travel with you and your child. Depending on her personal situation, she may or may not be able to leave the area where she lives. For instance, if the nanny candidate works additional hours at another job, she may be committed to those responsibilities.

The nanny may also have a fear or dislike of certain forms of transportation that may be necessary for you to reach your destination. Ask her up front if she is comfortable traveling by plane, train, boat, or whatever transportation is required. You do not want to get into a situation where you are taking care of both your child and your nanny during your travels.

If your nanny is assisting you with packing for your child, be sure to tell her to include any special toys or garments that may be needed at the destination. For example, if you are traveling to a beach community, make sure you bring your child's sandals, swimsuit, hat, towel, sunscreen, sand bucket, and shovel. If snow is in the forecast, items such as snow boots, a warm jacket, hats, gloves, and long underwear should be packed.

Some fun yet compact items you may want your nanny to pack for your child to ensure an enjoyable trip include the following:

- books or electronic reading devices
- child-friendly maps and destination highlight books
- easy art projects (sticker mosaics, beads and string, decorate-your-own postcard)
- crayons and coloring books
- inflatable toys (such as beach balls) that can be used outside or for bath toys
- flash cards
- travel-sized games such as chess, tangrams, or Mancala
- puzzles
- playing cards

- dice
- journals and colorful pens
- small scrapbooks and glue sticks or tape to document highlights from the trip
- educational workbooks
- stackable cups or blocks
- teething rings or teething toys

Once you reach your destination, try to replicate your home setup in order to get back into your child's routine. Designate certain areas or rooms for eating, playing, sleeping, and bathing. Make sure the appropriate supplies are available so that the nanny can execute her job flawlessly while your child has his or her needs met.

Provide your nanny with appropriate sleeping accommodations as well as snacks and meals (or money so she can get her own food). Do not assume that your nanny knows the area or has the time to research eating establishments while also taking care of your child. Give her a list of places to go for food or menus from establishments that provide food delivery.

Additionally, provide a list of activities the nanny may want to do with your child. Make your nanny aware of any interesting museum exhibits, local playgrounds, or fun shops your child might enjoy.

At a local Manhattan playground, one New-York-City-based mother met a Los-Angeles-based nanny who was traveling with a family from California. The California child had a great time running in the sprinklers while wearing her bathing suit and sunglasses. The nanny even had bubbles and a few water toys for her to play with at the playground. The NYC mother was amazed after talking to the LA nanny. She had taken the initiative to ask her hotel concierge where all the local parks and playgrounds were so the child could play while the parents were at business meetings.

A little resourcefulness goes a long way in terms of your child's joy while traveling.

Question: What are your expectations in terms of pay?
Follow-up: What amount of money have you received in the past from other families?

Compensation is often an awkward topic to discuss, but if your interview is going well, you may want to address it up front. You should have an idea of what you are willing to pay the nanny for her services before you enter into compensation discussions with her. Wages vary greatly across geographic regions. If you are unsure what pay is appropriate for your nanny, it is a good idea to ask your close neighbors, friends, or family members what they pay their nannies. Or call a local nanny-employment agency, financial professional, or employment attorney to find out the going rate for childcare in your area.

You should consider the following when thinking about nanny compensation:

- How many children do you have? (Volume discounts usually do not apply to nanny care.)
- How many hours will the nanny work per day/week?
- Is there a certain rate you want to set?
- Will the nanny work nontraditional hours?
- Which days of the week will the nanny be paid?
- What will you need to pay for overtime—additional hours from the agreed-upon level?
- Will you provide the nanny with certain snacks or meals?
- Will you pay for the nanny's further education, such as CPR classes and childcare seminars?
- Will you also pay for the nanny's transportation to or from your home?
- Will you pay for late-night or off-hours transportation for your nanny to get to her home?
- Will you give the nanny a raise for good performance?
- Will you give the nanny a yearly bonus for good performance?

Would you ask your surgeon for a discount on a knee operation? Of course not. So, do not try to be cheap when it comes to paying your nanny. Make sure you are paying the nanny a fair rate that you can afford. If the nanny feels like she is treated fairly in terms of compensation, then she is more likely to remain employed with your family if it is the right fit.

Giving your nanny the afternoon off (with pay) or coming home early and allowing her to leave your home ahead of schedule are examples of little ways you can reward your nanny for her childcare efforts and create goodwill. Additionally, if you give her a few surprise breaks, she may be more flexible when you need her to stay later one evening or work a few additional hours on the weekend.

If your nanny is doing a great job with your child, you may also want to supplement her compensation with other rewards as tokens of your appreciation.

Do you get excited when you are presented with an unexpected gift? Of course you do! It is always fun to get a little something when you least expect it. Nanny rewards may be big or small, but if they are well thought out, they are impactful and appreciated by the nanny recipient.

So feel free to shower your nanny with a surprise gift once in a while to reward her for a job well done. A little bottle of lotion for her work anniversary, a wallet for her birthday, or a sweater for the holidays would brighten up your nanny's day.

You could also have your child present the gift to your nanny. By encouraging your child to give a gift to your nanny, you are teaching the child to express gratitude at an early age.

One mother noticed her nanny loved wearing flip-flops both inside and outside the house. So, when the summertime weather kicked in, she gave her nanny a brand-new pair of pink flip-flops as a small but sweet thank-you gesture for taking such great care of her child.

A father observed that his nanny loved to use reusable cotton shopping bags. The father often attended industry conferences as part of his job, and many times canvas bags were given out to commemorate these events. After attending a few conferences, he brought a few bags home and presented them to his nanny to show his appreciation for her efforts. She was touched by his sincere expression of gratitude.

Here are some examples of nanny rewards:

- gift certificates for coffee, meals, books, music, clothing, movies
- spill-proof beverage containers
- clothing items
- scarves
- hats
- sunglasses
- bags, wallets, purses
- lotions or soaps
- a framed or gift-wrapped craft project that your child created
- photo albums or scrapbooks
- stationery or boxes of cards
- ornaments or holiday decorations
- key chains
- vases
- flowers
- health-club memberships
- vouchers for airline tickets
- magazine subscriptions

The more you get to know your nanny and her interests, the better you can tailor her gifts.

Question: Are you interested in working in our home on a part-time basis?
Follow-up: Are you comfortable with our house rules?

You and your partner deserve a break once in a while. Whether you need to shop for new tile for your bathroom, exercise to align your mind/body/spirit, participate in a fun-filled adult-only culinary class, enjoy yourselves at a friend's party, or watch the latest movie on a "date night," you will need to hire a babysitter for your child.

Part-time babysitters may be family members, neighbors (adult or teenaged students), current or former teachers (children love seeing their teachers in their own home), or referrals from friends. Whatever the case, these part-time babysitters are usually paid on an agreed-upon hourly rate and may or may not come to your home on a consistent basis. Thus, you should feel comfortable in setting ground rules up front and may want to remind the babysitters of your house rules when they arrive.

When it comes to laying the groundwork for your part-time babysitter, you may want to discuss the following:

- Do you want the babysitter answering the phone?
- Do you want the babysitter answering the doorbell?
- What can the child eat and drink? What can the babysitter eat and drink?
- Does the babysitter need to help the child with anything specific—such as brushing teeth, using the bathroom, helping with homework, or getting to bed?
- Does the babysitter know where the fire extinguisher is located?
- Does the babysitter know where the first-aid kit is located?
- Can the child have screen time (movies, computers, phones, other electronic devices)? Also, be clear if you do not want the babysitter on her personal electronic devices while your child is awake or at all.
- What the babysitter should do if the child falls ill with an earache, stomachache, sore throat, vomiting, and so on.
- Can the babysitter administer medicine to the child?

It is always a good idea to tell the babysitter when you will be home as well as give her the contact information on where you will be while she is caring for your child. As a courtesy, ask the babysitter if it is OK if you run late if you are going to an event that may not have a firm ending time. Additionally, parents should prepare "crib" notes that detail important information about the child/children as well as emergency contact information.

Babysitter's "Crib" Notes

Name, ages, and dates of birth of your children:

Allergy information/medications:

Eating/snacking routine:

Bedtime routine (time and instructions):

Other important information (including screen-time rules, homework, favorite games or books, fun activities, and so on):

Parental information
Home address (including apartment number and cross streets):

Home phone number:

Parent #1 name and work/cell phone number:

Parent #2 name and work/cell phone number:

Location of parents (including contact names/address/phone numbers):

Emergency information
Emergency contact:

Closest neighbor's contact:

Pediatrician's number and address:

Dentist's number and address:

Hospital's number and address:

Poison-control number:

If there is an emergency please call 911 first and then call parents!

CHAPTER 3

Punctuality, Transportation, Vacations: Clear Expectations

● ● ●

WHETHER IT IS YOUR TIME or your nanny's time, a clear understanding of your expectations and your nanny's needs is essential. It is important to make sure that your nanny has the same expectations for punctuality and time management as you do. Parents also need to be punctual so that nannies can meet their other obligations.

Question: Are you a punctual person?

Follow-up: Can you please contact us if you are running late or unable to work?

Anyone who has ever held a job realizes the importance of showing up to work on time and ready to perform. Nannies are no exception to these workplace rules and should be held to those same standards.

You should communicate to the nanny candidate that she must try her best to be punctual. Tell her that she is part of a team and if she can please respect your time by being prompt to work, then you promise to do the same and get home by the agreed-upon time.

Delays, accidents, or traffic jams are not always easy to avoid, so let your nanny know that if she is running late for any reason, you would like her to please give you a call, send you an e-mail, or shoot you a text. (It is best to agree upon a preferred method of communication). In return, you must provide the same courtesy with your nanny and contact her if you are delayed.

Vacation and sick days (as well as related compensation) should be decided and detailed up front. You do not want your nanny crawling to work when she is running a high fever, vomiting, or dealing with pinkeye or strep throat. Your child's health and well-being (not to mention that of your nanny) are more important than anything you may have planned that day. However, if you notice a pattern of absences with your nanny, then confront her right away to see if there is an issue that needs to be addressed or a backup childcare plan that should be implemented.

Let your nanny know that if she cannot come to work on a certain day, she should try to give you advance notice so you can arrange backup childcare if possible. In an ideal world, you should have at least three levels of backup childcare in case your nanny cannot work on a day that you or your partner has an important meeting, presentation, or task. Backup childcare examples may include the following:

- you
- your partner

- a nearby friend or neighbor
- a close relative
- another nanny or babysitter who has a flexible schedule
- a drop-in day-care center

Some employers have backup childcare services available for families who may find themselves in a pinch. You and your partner should check out your firm's childcare offerings and policies. In many situations where backup childcare is offered by an employer, the parents must fill out paperwork in advance to register the child. Additionally, the child's doctor may also have to fill out paperwork to answer questions relating to the child's medical history.

Also, keep in mind that the childcare offering may not be located at your office. Instead, it might be at a childcare facility in another location. Some backup childcare facilities are available to families on a first-come, first-served basis and may fill up quickly. Make sure that you know about all the rules and paperwork involved with your firm's backup childcare before you need to use it for your child.

Question: Do you feel comfortable transporting our child, and can you do so safely?

Follow-up: Will you respect our geographic boundaries when transporting our child?

You and your partner should discuss and decide what methods of transportation you are comfortable with when your nanny has to transport your child. Here are examples:

- her car
- your car
- bus
- subway
- train
- taxi
- ferry
- walking (possibly with a stroller)
- bicycles
- scooters

If you expect the nanny to drive your child to various activities or educational events, make sure you ask her about her driving status. You may want to limit how far she travels with your child (distance) and make her aware of dangerous roads or intersections. Additionally, it is a nice idea to educate her on the area you live in as well as the places she may frequent with your child. Do not expect or encourage your nanny to take your child out in a car when the weather is bad.

Also, decide if the nanny will use a car that you provide or her own car. You and your nanny should discuss gasoline and maintenance expenses and reimbursement procedures up front. You do not want your nanny to run out of gas with your child in the car and to feel stranded or helpless.

If you live in a city, decide what types of public transportation are acceptable for your nanny to take with your child. If train, subway, or bus schedules are confusing or unreliable, then map out specific times of travel and routes to travel and review them with your nanny. Figure out the cost involved, and either prepay these travel expenses or reimburse her once the activity is completed.

Tell the nanny if she should avoid any particular areas or streets. Additionally, let the nanny know if any areas are particularly dangerous. Whether you live in the city, suburbs, or a rural community, it is a wise idea to set specific geographic boundaries for driving as well as walking with a stroller.

Question: Would you provide us with a list of vacation days in advance?
Follow-up: Can you please let us know in advance about any special days you need to arrive late or leave early?

Respect your nanny and let her know far in advance (if possible) when you will be on vacation or taking a day off and do not need her to work. Ask her to give you the same courtesy of advance notice regarding the days she needs off. Remember, you and your nanny are a team, and if backup child care is necessary, you need to be prepared.

Some families work with their nannies to coordinate vacation schedules, so either limited or no backup childcare is needed. At the beginning of each year, one set of parents and their nanny sat down with pocket calendars and planned all of their vacation days/weeks for the upcoming year. The nanny felt as if she was not only a part of the family, but also an influential party in the decision-making process. As she was a grandmother herself, she was able to book her flights to see her friends and family far in advance. The parents were thrilled that they were able to agree on most of the same vacation days with their nanny and only needed to make limited arrangements for backup care.

One mother who worked a flexible schedule encouraged her nanny to give her advance warning of days needed off for personal days so that she could work around the nanny's absence. Because much of the mother's work was project or freelance oriented, she would have her nanny work longer days (and pay her accordingly) leading up to the days the nanny would have off in order to meet her deadlines. The nanny was happy to get a little extra spending money, too.

In addition to preplanning vacation days, you and your nanny should discuss any late arrivals or early departures needed. Depending on the situation, you may have to arrange for backup childcare if she has an obligation during the hours she normally works with your family. Additionally, you may have an early morning or late afternoon appointment and may need to ask her if it is possible to adjust her schedule. Depending on the situation, you may want to do something extra special if she does alter her schedule to suit your needs. A simple act of kindness goes a long way in your relationship with your caregiver.

CHAPTER 4

Motivation, Desire, Character: Nanny Management

● ● ●

FROM DAY ONE, YOUR NANNY must respect you and what you determine are the main priorities for her while she is taking care of your child. You want to be sure to hire a nanny with good character. Additionally, you want a nanny who has the motivation to honor your priorities.

Question: What do you consider to be the ideal priorities for a nanny?
Follow-up: Why would you consider yourself an ideal nanny?

You and your partner should compose a list of what you believe to be the ideal priorities for your nanny. Think about the characteristics, personality traits, tasks, and responsibilities you expect of your nanny, and prioritize them.

Asking your nanny candidate these questions will enable her to give you her perspective on what she believes it means to be a nanny. It opens up a discussion between you and the nanny candidate regarding the aspects of her job that are most important. You want to walk away from the interview feeling that she has a thorough understanding of what the job entails. Additionally, you want to see if she feels confident in her abilities to excel as your nanny.

You also want to get an idea of her judgment. It is important to let her know that you do not expect her to take on several tasks simultaneously. For instance, be clear that your child's safety comes before any cleaning tasks. Obviously, the child's meals are a priority over fun activities such as art projects or physical play.

Once you create your own "Pyramid of Nanny Priorities," you may want to show it to your nanny and discuss its contents. Make sure she understands and respects what you view to be the top priorities for her while she is taking care of your child. Ask her if she wants to add anything to the pyramid that she feels is important. It is very important to keep the communication lines flowing so that you develop mutual admiration and respect.

Pyramid of Nanny Priorities

Communication,
Safety, Trust

Responsible, Intelligent,
Loyal, Dedicated

Motivated, Understanding,
Respectful

Prompt, Patient, Cheerful

Clean, Thorough, Creative

Handles daily routine/tasks (meal or bottle
preparation, eating and sleeping schedules)

Actively engages the child (reading, art
projects, music, classes, physical and developmental play)

Happily takes on additional agreed upon
responsibilities for the child (cleaning, laundry, errands)

Question: What words can be used to describe you?
Follow-up: What are some of your shortcomings?

If you ask the nanny to talk about her personality, characteristics, and traits, you are allowing her to open up to you. You could also ask her references the same questions and see if you get similar answers.

These questions are best asked during a face-to-face interview where you can witness her expressions. Do her actions seem to match her words? Pay careful attention to the words she uses to describe herself, and ask her questions to expand upon her answers. For instance, if she says she is intelligent, then ask her for an example of how she used her intelligence in a childcare situation. Examples may include helping to teach the child something new or acting quickly in an emergency situation.

Positive adjectives/words you want to listen for include the following:

- cheerful
- sweet
- fun
- happy
- loving
- kind
- gentle
- motivated
- smart
- careful
- thoughtful
- understanding
- nurturing
- detailed
- loyal
- dedicated
- committed
- organized

- healthy
- active
- energetic
- playful
- creative
- clean
- trustworthy
- patient
- helpful
- mature
- experienced
- articulate
- tolerant
- respectful
- safe
- prompt
- thorough

Many people only want to talk about their positive traits. But, you should always follow up with additional questions to delve into the nanny candidate's shortcomings or areas of weakness. If her responses concern you, then you should try to ask her follow-up questions to get her to elaborate on her choice of words. Perhaps ask her to give you some situational stories to allow her to further explain herself. After hearing her clarification, if you are still unhappy or uncomfortable for any reason, you may want to move to the next nanny candidate.

Negative adjectives/words you may hear include the following:

- impatient
- stressed
- flaky
- rushed
- short-tempered

- angry
- unreliable
- pessimistic
- irresponsible
- stubborn
- noncommittal
- cynical
- naïve
- pompous
- distracted
- dependent
- dramatic
- judgmental
- nervous
- tired
- intolerant
- picky
- risky
- lazy
- careless
- moody

Sit down with your partner and create a list of words that you believe describe the ideal nanny for your child. Keep this list with you when you interview nannies and make notes as the interview proceeds. This will help you to evaluate the candidates who best fit your expectations.

If you have a gut feeling that the nanny candidate is stubborn or lacks patience, then she should not be your child's nanny. Your child deserves to be taken care of by someone who is nurturing and patient. Children are smart and can sense when an adult is not in a good mood. You want to create a loving, caring, and gentle environment for your child.

Question: Are you nurturing?
Follow-up: Provide an example of a situation when you felt you nurtured a child.

During an interview, it may be hard to judge if the nanny candidate is nurturing. If you have a young baby, then toward the end of the interview, hand the baby over to the nanny candidate and watch how they both respond. Watch her interact with your baby, and take note of her demeanor.

- Did the nanny ask to wash her hands or use hand sanitizer before holding the baby?
- Are you comfortable with the way the nanny supported your baby's head and neck?
- Does the nanny seem gentle?
- Can the nanny comfort the child?
- Do her movements seem natural?
- Is she tender?
- Does she look directly into the child's eyes?
- Does she seem to respect the child?
- Does she hug or kiss the child?

If you have an older child, you should ask the nanny candidate to interact with him or her by playing a game she is familiar with or doing an art project. Once again, see how she acts around your child and evaluate whether she would be a good fit.

- Does she engage your child in lively conversation?
- Does she clearly explain the rules of the game or the instructions of the art project?
- Does she seem patient?
- Does she answer your child's questions in a clear and pleasant manner?
- Does she encourage your child in a positive way?

You should also watch for any negative interactions between the nanny candidate and child.

- Does she seem unnatural?
- Does she seem scared?
- Does she seem timid?
- Does she seem insecure?
- Does she seem phony?
- Does she seem impatient?

One mother who had lost her own mother at a young age instantly viewed the nanny candidate as a natural with her child. She was greatly impressed with how she held and cuddled her baby. After a few years, the mother now views the nanny as a mother figure for herself and a grandmother figure for her child.

Another parent summed up his expectations for the ideal nanny like this: "I don't want to find a mother or a grandmother to care for my child. I want to find an aunt." He believed there was nobody who could replace his child's own mother or grandmothers. However, he thought that someone with experience could perhaps combine the energy of a mother with the wisdom of a grandmother.

Question: Do you believe you have good judgment?

Follow-up: Please provide an example of how you used good judgment while taking care of a child.

Good judgment and the ability to make rational, wise decisions can be hard to assess in an interview.

One mother worked alongside her nanny in order to train her for a full two weeks before her maternity leave expired. The nanny arrived at the mother's home promptly each morning so the mother could teach her the baby's routine each day. The mother showed the nanny where everything was kept, how to make and sterilize the bottles, where to look for extra or emergency supplies, and so on. The mother stressed how important it was to engage the baby with music, books, toys, or tummy-time activities. Additionally, the mother provided the nanny with a list of house rules including no TV when the baby was awake. The family did not want the baby plopped in front of a TV screen all day long without human interaction.

Toward the end of the mother's first week back at the office, she decided to make a surprise (read: "unannounced") visit to check up on her baby. One Friday, around lunchtime she hopped on the subway, stopped for a falafel, and entered her apartment building, feeling extremely excited to see her baby at midday.

As she exited the elevator, she heard a TV blaring from one of the apartment units on her side of the building. She muttered under her breath about how disrespectful it was to leave a TV on so loudly and decided she might have to voice her complaint to the building's super. However, the sounds of the TV got louder and her annoyance increased as she approached her apartment unit. She put the key in the door to find her baby by herself. Her child was on the sofa propped up on a pillow in front of the family's glass coffee table. The noon news was blaring details of a wild police chase, and no nanny was in sight.

She quickly scooped up her precious bundle of joy as the nanny came out of the bathroom shrieking that she never left the baby there but had to use the bathroom for a minute. And she continued to say that she never watched TV but wanted to see one news story.

The trust had been broken. Numerous rules had been broken. The baby had been put into danger. The nanny should have put the baby in a safe location (such as a crib) when she went to the bathroom, and the TV was not supposed to be turned on during the day. The mother paid the nanny what she was owed, and the nanny was replaced.

Evaluating someone's judgment during the interview process may be tricky. You will likely have to go with your gut feeling after meeting the candidate. It is a good idea to make unannounced visits from time to time. Also, ask others who may be around your baby and nanny how they think the relationship is working.

One working mother was approached in the park on the weekend by another mother, who told her that she had observed the family's nanny and believed her to be neglectful of the children. The mother promptly installed a video camera (always check with an attorney about current laws in your area before the installation of such devices). After watching endless amounts of video, she decided the other mother had correctly assessed the situation. Through the tapes, she saw the nanny on her cell phone for large amounts of time—during meals and while "playing" with the children. Additionally, she noticed her child was placed in her crib far too often and ignored for long durations. She realized she needed to address the concerns and eventually found a replacement.

Question: Are you a neat person?
Follow-up: Will you either wash my child's hands or make sure my child washes his or her own hands every time he or she comes in from outside the home as well as before all meals?

Remember, at the first meeting, the nanny candidate does not know any of your house rules regarding cleanliness. Observe her actions and keep track of the following:

- Did she take her shoes off when she entered your home?
- Did she wash her hands upon entering your home?
- Did she ask where you keep hand sanitizer in all of your rooms?

Most nanny candidates want to make a good first impression, so the serious ones may display their penchant for cleanliness. You may be surprised by a nanny candidate who notices and points out any bugs, mold, or dust in your home in your first meeting. Moreover, it could be a good sign if she asks you where you keep your basic cleaning supplies in case of a spill.

If the nanny candidate does not automatically do any of the above things to display her cleanliness or other things that you deem important, then ask her to take off her shoes, wash her hands, or whatever else you feel is appropriate and see how she responds. Is she apologetic, defensive, or compliant?

One mother of young children was completely disturbed at the nanny candidate's stubbornness when she asked her to wash her hands before touching the children. The nanny snapped at the mother by telling her that not only has she been a mother herself but also a nanny for several years, and all the children under her care turned out fine. Needless to say, as a result of her poor attitude and disrespect of household rules, she did not get the job.

It is perfectly fair for you to lay out to your nanny rules that everyone who enters your home (including all family members) must abide by in order to keep the home sanitary. It is easiest to follow rules if the process to do so is fun, as in these examples:

- Take a colorful basket or large container, label it "shoes," and place it at your front door for everyone to use when they enter your home.
- Make the handwashing process enjoyable by offering a selection of colorful, fragrant, antibacterial soaps or lotions and plush hand towels in your kitchen and bathrooms.
- Buy different-colored hand sanitizers for the various rooms in your home to keep the procedure enjoyable. Not to mention, it is hard for people to forget to sanitize their hands when bright pink or green hand sanitizer is right in front of their eyes.

Question: What are your extracurricular activities?
Follow-up: What are some of your hobbies?

Although asking the nanny candidate about her favorite extracurricular activities or hobbies may sound like a pickup line at a cocktail party, the response may provide you with insight into what kind of person she is when she is not caring for your child.

For instance, one mother was elated when the nanny candidate expressed a passion for reading and learning. The nanny further explained that her goal was to save enough money to be able to attend college and earn a degree in nursing with a specialty in pediatrics. The nanny took interest in the child's book collection and even made a few suggestions for new additions to the family's home library.

If your nanny enjoys reading in her free time, then by all means encourage her to bring the love of her hobby into your home by reading to or with your child on a frequent basis. She may also know libraries, bookstores, or children's centers that have the best story-time hour. The nanny who loves to read may even expose your child to new authors, books, or publications.

Conversely, a red light may pop up if the nanny admits to participating in something that compromises the values of your family. For instance, if the nanny admits she is a shopaholic, it may be a cause for concern. You do not want your child to be dragged from store to store or dressing room to dressing room while the nanny is caring for him or her. Make sure you are clear that personal shopping should be limited to her hours outside of work. Stress that she should not use the time you are paying her for shopping excursions or errands for herself.

Sometimes you can turn a potentially negative situation into a positive one. If you want to leverage her zest for shopping, you can give her a list of items you need for your child along with the appropriate money. You might ask her to go shopping for the following types of items:

- milk or formula
- baby/child food or snacks

- pharmacy items
- diapers, wipes, cream, or ointment
- specific children's books
- developmental toys
- games
- children's clothing items or accessories
- seasonal items for your child
- back-to-school supplies
- tools for arts and crafts
- vacation needs
- birthday presents for your child or his or her friends

Be sure to tell her exactly where to go for the items and how much to spend and that you do not expect her to deviate from your shopping list.

Question: Are you a festive person?
Follow-up: How would you help a child get into the celebratory spirit?

Celebrations and parties can be fun for everyone. If your nanny does like festivities, then encourage her to involve your child in seasonally appropriate activities or projects. These projects do not have to be creatively intensive or religious in nature (you should not ask the nanny candidate about religious views, customs, or holidays). The projects should be simple yet fun for everyone.

Some examples of fun, festive, seasonal projects that your nanny can do with your child include the following:

- rolling dough, baking, and decorating cookies or cakes
- creating special cards
- making gifts for family members, friends, teachers, or neighbors
- creating wrapping paper or gift bags from everyday materials around the home
- decorating pumpkins with paint or glitter
- making flags or wind chimes
- engaging in seasonal projects
- designing ice skates using colored paper or fabric in the winter months
- pressing leaves in the fall
- creating flower arrangements in the spring
- making sand projects in the summer
- creating a concert or play for the child's parents in your home
- listening to music and singing along
- reading or creating seasonally appropriate books
- making handprints to give to the parents on special days
- building cakes from blocks
- creating wreaths
- working on seasonal dioramas out of old shoe boxes

One busy mother was deeply touched when her nanny showed up at her home with a bag full of supplies for her son's first birthday. Previously, the mother had told the nanny that because most relatives lived out of the area, she would just make a cake and hold a simple first birthday party for her son with both parents and the nanny as the guests. The nanny wanted to make the child's first birthday a very special occasion for the family, so she surprised the family by contributing colorful paper plates, napkins, and a tablecloth to the small party. The mother was so thankful that she had thought of these small yet important details. The nanny was very happy that she was able to be a part of the festivities.

Another mother was thrilled with the ex-preschool teacher she had as her child's nanny. She greatly appreciated her nanny's enthusiasm for celebrations, not to mention her creative spirit. She was absolutely impressed with the way the nanny carried her excitement to the child every single day. The nanny helped the child make pumpkins in the fall, snowflakes in the winter, tulips in the spring, and sailboats in the summer. Depending on the season, the windows were beautifully decorated with paper flowers, bells, hearts, rainbows, snowmen, leaves, or trees.

Question: Are you used to caring for children who are extremely active?
Follow-up: Can you deal with a child who may have to be carried or pushed in a stroller?

You have to be careful when asking nanny candidates about their age and health. For further clarification, you may want to investigate whether your line of questioning is legal. Consult an employment lawyer or agency before asking such questions. Such professionals can give you guidelines on how to deal with questions relating to these topics.

You may want to tell the nanny candidate if your child is extremely active. Also, let the nanny candidate know if your child is young and may have to be carried or pushed in a stroller from time to time after long walks in the park or a busy day at school. It is important to lay out the specific responsibilities you expect of the nanny. The more detailed you are, the better she will understand the demands of the role with you family. And, do not do all the talking. Let her ask you as many questions as she wants. Answer them honestly and with details. You do not want the nanny to be surprised about the job functions that she may need to perform. Additionally, you want to make sure the nanny candidate can perform job assignments safely.

Question: Are you comfortable working for a family who follows certain religious practices?

Follow-up: Would you help drop off our child at religion classes?

Although you should not ask the nanny candidate about her religious views, you can talk to her about your family's religious practices, if applicable.

Your children may have to attend religious-education classes, and sometimes your nanny may be responsible for dropping them off and picking them up from your place of worship. You should explain to the nanny candidate what is expected of her, and make sure she is comfortable with the responsibilities. If your religion requires you to observe certain practices in your kitchen, it is best to lay out this practice to the nanny candidate so she understands its importance.

If it is critical to you that your child builds a foundation to respect and appreciate all religions, then communicate that to your nanny up front. Tell your nanny that your family has certain beliefs, but it is OK if your child is exposed to other religions at playdates, holiday parties, or dinners. You may feel that it is good for your child to experience how others view spirituality as it may make your child a more well-rounded and accepting individual.

If the nanny candidate expresses discomfort with your religious views or practices inside or outside your home, then respect her opinion as she may not be the right nanny candidate for your family. If your religious beliefs are too different from the nanny's, then nobody will be happy with the situation.

CHAPTER 5

House Rules, Daily Routine, Chores, Grooming: Structuring the Job

● ● ●

WHEN ALL IS SAID AND done, being a nanny is a job. Like any job, there are rules, routines to follow, and tasks that must be performed.

Question: Will you abide by our house rules?
Follow-up: Do you have issues with any of these rules?

Be straightforward when you provide a list of the rules of your house. Giving rules verbally is fine, but providing written rules is recommended, as there is often a lot of information to absorb. Do not assume the nanny candidate knows how you run your household.

For example, make it clear that there may be some things you don't want your child to do, but these things may be fine for the nanny to do (such as drink caffeinated beverages or chew gum). You may have some things that are forbidden items in your household (fast food or gummy candies).

Evaluate what is important to you, and communicate it to your nanny. You may never give your one-year-old ice cream, but of course, you may eat it from time to time. And you may even keep it in your house for your nanny to indulge in when the child's asleep or at school. If your family does not drink soda but you have no problem buying it for your nanny who really enjoys it, then make it clear to the nanny that it is off-limits to the child.

Here are examples of house rules for your nanny:

PLEASE DO

- Read to the child and try to keep her engaged in all activities.
- Interact with the child.
- Sing songs to the child or play the music we provide (such as classical, seasonal, or other children's music).
- Talk to the child even if it is as simple as describing what you are doing (it helps to build her vocabulary).
- Play with the child in a gentle manner (age-appropriate play may include offering tummy time on an activity mat, having tea parties with dolls, working on puzzles, playing dress-up, creating buildings with blocks, or playing board games).

- Engage the child in art projects with the supplies we provide (crayons, finger paint, play dough, clay, felt, and so on).
- Use proper manners (please, thank you), and teach our child to do so as well.
- Wash your hands before handling the child.
- Encourage healthy eating habits.
- Help the child with grooming.
- Keep us aware of anything special or unusual that happens in the child's day when we are not around.

PLEASE DO NOT

- Do not shake our child.
- Do not use blankets in our child's crib.
- Do not watch television when the child is awake.
- Do not use foul language.
- Do not shout or yell.
- Do not spank or hit our child. (Time-outs or another agreed-upon method can be used to reprimand the child for wrongdoings.)
- Do not talk, e-mail, or text constantly on the phone; please limit your phone usage for emergencies or calling us to check in.
- Do not wear shoes inside the home (slippers are fine).
- Do not wear strong perfume in our home (if your baby has allergies or sensitive skin).
- Do not take the child swimming or near pools or open water unless cleared by us.
- Do not eat certain unhealthy foods in front of the child.
- Do not feed the children fast food or candy (unless he or she is attending a birthday or other party).
- Do not use pacifiers for the child.

Create and organize a folder for your nanny so she has critical information all in one place. Keep this folder in a visible place, as she'll refer to it each time she enters your home.

You can even make it a fun project by decorating a three-ring binder for your nanny and creating colorful tabs for various types of information such as these:

- Tab A: Important Contact Information
- Tab B: Nanny's Responsibilities
- Tab C: Daily Log (enough for the upcoming week or month)
- Tab D: Activity Calendar
- Tab E: List for the Diaper Bag
- Tab F: Any relevant articles, medical journals, and doctor's pamphlets you believe might be helpful for your nanny to read and review

Tab A. Contact Information/Emergencies

It is critical that you review important contact information with your nanny in the event of an emergency. Place a copy of your family's contact information along with a CPR "cheat sheet" in a highly visible place in your home such as on the refrigerator, near the entrance, or by the phone. Also, place copies in your "nanny folder" as well as in the child's diaper bag. In addition, make sure to give a copy of this contact information to your nanny for her safekeeping. You may also want to provide your nanny with access to "emergency" money in a sealed envelope placed in a drawer, the diaper bag, or on the refrigerator. This money can be used for gas or cab fare to the doctor's office or to buy necessary supplies. By taking these precautions, you are ensuring that your child will get the attention he or she deserves and needs in the shortest amount of time in case of an emergency.

IMPORTANT CONTACT INFORMATION

Child's name:

Child's date of birth:

Child's allergies or other issues:

Child's blood type/medications:

Child's home phone number:

Child's home street address (including apartment number):

Apartment-building doorman's phone number:

Mother's name _____ Work phone number ___ Cell-phone number___
Father's name_____ Work phone number ___ Cell-phone number ___

Pediatrician: Dr. ____
Office address:
Office phone number:

Dentist: Dr. ____
Office address:
Office phone number:

Person in case of emergency _____ Phone number _____

*Note: Contact information is also in the child's diaper bag and posted _____.

For Emergencies:

If the child is in danger (injured, choking, unconscious, poisoned, or anything else out of the ordinary) please call 911 for emergency, then call us (Mom or Dad).

Emergency: 911
Poison Control Hotline: 1-800-222-1222

Tab B. Nanny's Responsibilities (Example For A Female Child)

PLEASE DO

- Read to our child. She has many books. Keep her engaged. We try to keep children's books in the bookshelves in each of our rooms.
- Point out interesting things to our child that you notice and appreciate in museums or libraries or outdoors. Please interact with our child to keep her interested and engaged.
- Sing to or with our child, as she loves music. You could put on a children's CD, too.
- Play games with our child. She likes to dress up, too!
- Talk to our child constantly, and ask her thoughtful questions.

PLEASE DO NOT

- Never leave our child unattended (inside or outside our home).
- Never put on the TV when our child is awake.
- Please do not chat or text on your cell phone unless necessary (or unless we are calling)—especially when pushing the stroller outside or driving.

DAILY ROUTINE

When our child comes home from an activity, please make sure she washes her hands upon entering the front door. If the child has stains on her clothing, please remove them and put fresh clothing on the child. Then, you can head to the bathroom, clean the stain, and place the soiled clothing over the shower rod in the bathroom.

If you notice our child has outgrown clothing, socks, or shoes, please let us know.

If she gets a scratch or cuts herself, please use ointment that we provide on the areas that look irritated. Additionally, our first-aid kit is underneath the sink in the main bathroom if you need it.

In the summer, please put sunscreen on our child before taking her out. Encourage her to wear sunglasses and a sunhat.

In the winter, make sure our child has a sweater, warm jacket, hat, mittens, and boots if she goes outside.

After you feed her dinner, please assist our child with brushing her teeth before helping her with her nighttime bath. If we are not home for bedtime, please read a book to her.

Tab C. Daily Log

CHILD'S DAILY LOG (TO BE FILLED IN BY NANNY)

Mother
Work Phone   Cell Phone Number
Father
Work Phone Number   Cell Phone Number

Person In Case of Emergency
Phone Number

Dr's Name
Dr's Office Phone Number

Child's Name
Child's Date of Birth
Child's Allergies or other Issues

DAILY LOG
DATE

FEEDING AND DIAPER LOG

Start Time	Finish Time	Burps	Ounces	Wet Diaper	Soiled Diaper	Notes

SLEEP LOG

Time Fell Asleep	Time Awoke	Notes

Activities with Child	Time	Notes
Activity Mat		
Tummy Time		
Reading Books		
Singing/Music		
Stroller Rides		
Art Projects		
Playground/Park		
Other		

Other To Do:	Time	Notes
Sterilize Bottles		
Prepare Bottles		
Prepare Food		
Other		

Notes (please detail anything you believe the parents should know):

Tab D: Activity Calendar

(Display in a prominent spot such as the refrigerator or a bulletin board and keep a copy in the diaper bag.)

	Sunday	Monday	Tuesday	Wednesday	Thursday	Friday	Saturday
5:00 AM							
6:00 AM							
7:00 AM							
8:00 AM							
9:00 AM							Swim Class with Child/Parents
10:00 AM		Art Class					
11:00 AM				Playdate			
12 NOON							
1:00 PM						Storytime Hour at Library	
2:00 PM					Music Class		
3:00 PM			Open Gym for Kids				
4:00 PM							
5:00 PM							
6:00 PM							
7:00 PM							
8:00 PM							
9:00 PM							

Special Events:

February 14th	Parent/Child Valentine's Day Dance
June 21st	Summertime Parks and Recreation Clean-Up Volunteer Event for Families
September 4th	Back to School Kick-Off Lunch in the Park
October 31st	Halloween Parade
December 15th	Holiday Concert

Tab E: List for the Diaper Bag

Most mothers or fathers can tell you of at least one time in their child's lives when they were away from home and did not have the proper supplies.

One mother took her child to the zoo and discovered that she had forgotten to bring an extra set of clothes. Unfortunately, the discovery took place after her child had leaked through her diaper near the zebras. Luckily, it was a rather warm day, so she was able to put a fresh diaper on her child and cover her bottom half with a blanket.

Do your nanny a favor, and try to keep your diaper bag well stocked with the necessities. You may ask her to replenish the supplies from your home stash, or just restock it yourself.

Your child's diaper bag may include the following items (depending on his or her age):

- your child's emergency contact information sheet (physician's or dentist's names and phone numbers, allergy information, and so on)
- diapers in a reusable bag for protection
- travel-size wipes
- diaper-area cream or ointment
- hand sanitizer or disinfectant wipes
- diaper disposal bags (you can purchase environmentally friendly bags)
- small blanket
- changing pad
- small first-aid kit (adhesive bandages as well as antiseptic wash/ointment)
- small toys or books (teething rings, links, and so on)
- change of clothing (depending on the weather, a onesie and pajamas may do the trick)
- sunscreen
- sunglasses
- hat
- travel-size tissues

- travel-size petroleum jelly
- burp cloth
- bib
- food or snack in a secure bag or container
- bottle or sippy cup and accompanying beverage (water, milk, formula, juice) in a secure bag

In order to protect and organize your child's meals when he or she is out and about, you can use clear cosmetic bags with zippers to store all food items. One bag could store a few meals along with a bib and utensils. Additional bags can be used to store bottles for milk or water. You or your nanny just has to fill up the cosmetic bags and throw them into the child's diaper bag, and everyone is ready to go. You can also put these bags in your carry-on luggage when traveling by air (sans liquids). The child's meals will be organized, clean, and fresh. You could use additional bags to store diapers and cream as well as an extra set of clothing or even teething rings.

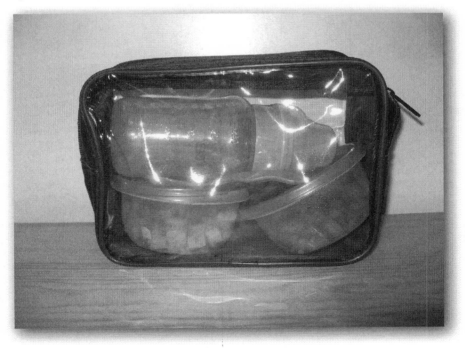

Tab F: Any Relevant Articles, Medical Journals, and Doctor's Pamphlets You Believe Might Be Helpful For Your Nanny to Read and Review

Your child's pediatrician may have some interesting articles or pamphlets for you and your nanny to read about developmental milestones or tips for a healthy lifestyle. Additionally, any time you see an interesting story in a magazine or newspaper, clip it out and place it in this tab for your nanny to read.

Question: Do you have any dietary restrictions or allergies that we should be aware of when you are in our house?

Follow-up: What do you like to eat or drink when taking care of a child?

Questions about dietary restrictions or eating habits could provide insight into what the nanny may expose your child to each day. If the nanny admits to frequenting fast-food restaurants, you will be prepared. It is totally reasonable to tell her that you do not want your child eating fast food (even nibbles). One mother told the nanny it was fine if she brought fast food into their house for herself, but she did not want her child to eat it, and she never wanted the child to step foot in a fast food restaurant. The mother cited her family history of heart disease and medical issues as the reason for banning fast food in her child's diet.

One working mother walked in on her newly hired nanny putting ice cream on top of meatloaf in an attempt to get the child to eat lunch. Utterly shocked, she calmly explained that meatloaf à la mode was an unacceptable meal and she hoped to never see such an action again. She told the nanny that she would rather her child not eat the served dish if he were not expressing a desire for meatloaf than be fed ice cream as part of an entrée and that the family always had other healthy meal options in the refrigerator.

If your nanny alerts you to any dietary restrictions, ask her how she wants to handle mealtime while she is working in your home. Perhaps she intends to bring in meals she has prepared in her own home. Or maybe she wants to provide you with a list of restricted food items as well as alternatives for you to buy and keep on hand for her snacks and meals. Obviously, if both your child and the nanny have a sensitivity or intolerance to gluten, it may not be a problem for you to buy extra gluten-free items for your pantry. However, depending on the specific dietary restriction or food allergy, it may be too time-consuming and expensive for you to provide her with specific food items. Just make sure you iron out these details early on so expectations are set in terms of food and beverage supply.

Health-conscious parents do not need to compromise their healthy beliefs while shopping for their nanny at the supermarket. You could ask the nanny more pointed questions that enable you to purchase healthy foods for both your family and the nanny, including the following:

- What are your favorite vegetables to snack on?
- What are your favorite fruits to snack on?
- What types of yogurt, cottage cheese, cereal, or nuts do you like?
- Do you like tap, flat, or sparkling water?
- What grain of bread or crackers do you like?

One mother sectioned off a portion of her cupboard for her nanny's food. She felt that if the nanny had her favorite foods in the child's home, she would feel like part of the family. The mother bought the nanny her favorite healthy snacks and replenished her portion of the cupboard on a regular basis.

Another mother noticed that her nanny always came with a fresh cup of coffee in the morning. She decided to provide that brand of coffee in her nanny's favorite flavor so the nanny could make it every morning in the family's kitchen. The mother joked that her nanny needed an extra jolt of energy each morning to take care of her active toddler.

Another mother was so happy to discover that her nanny was an amazing cook. Although the mother never specifically asked her to make meals for the family, the nanny would often bring the family containers of food that she had made at home the previous evening. The mother was thrilled that her child was expanding his palate by trying diverse foods from another culture. In fact, the mother and child enjoyed the nanny's food so much that she asked the nanny to make all of the food for her child's birthday party and paid her accordingly.

It is important that you find out right away if your nanny candidate has any allergies that you should be aware of while she is in your home. If she is comfortable sharing this information, you can plan accordingly. And, let her know if your child or any of your family members have any such restrictions. If your child does, indeed, have an allergy, show or tell her what to do in case of an allergic reaction. If an injection device is involved, then teach the nanny the importance of carrying it at all times (if necessary) and instruct her on how to use it in the event of an emergency.

Question: How do you feel about establishing and following daily eating and sleeping routines for the child?

Follow-up: Are you comfortable keeping track of daily activities in a logbook?

Some families run by routine, while others are more spontaneous in maintaining their household. If following a routine is critical to you and your family, you need to stress the importance of staying organized and on schedule to the nanny candidate. Additionally, be specific as to exactly what type of daily itinerary or schedule you expect the nanny to follow.

As previously mentioned, it is a good idea to create a daily log for recordkeeping that you can keep in your nanny's folder. Depending on how stringent you are with recordkeeping, you or your partner may want to have a mini-training session with your nanny to go over how to fill in the daily log sheets. Additionally, on the days you are at home with the children, you may want to fill in the daily logs so that your nanny can refer to them when she returns. Your notes will better enable the nanny to understand your child's routine. Please make the nanny aware that the daily logs are just one tool for recordkeeping, and tell her to let you know if she notices anything special or unusual about the child.

Milk or Formula

Most parents want to make sure their child is neither underfed nor over-fed. Many parents develop an eating schedule for their baby or toddler that may be altered as the child gets older.

For infants, it is important to keep track of how many ounces of milk or formula the baby consumes each day. Additionally, a lot of parents develop an eating schedule to make sure the child is getting the appropriate amount of milk or formula at specific times throughout the day. The parents and nanny should record what time the baby was fed and how many ounces the baby consumed. Many parents make their nanny aware that the baby does not need to completely finish each bottle. Moreover, the nanny should not force-feed the baby.

Additionally, explain the significance of burping the baby after feedings. Be specific with your nanny, and tell her how many burps your baby usually has after each bottle at feeding times. If your baby tends to spit up a lot, then make your nanny aware of that as well. Keep plenty of burp cloths in a visible spot so your nanny can use them throughout the day. Instruct your nanny to change the baby's clothing if he or she spits up on the garments.

Tell your nanny how many minutes she should hold your baby as part of the digesting period before she puts the baby down in a crib, in a stroller, on a blanket, or on an activity mat.

Solid Foods

If your child is eating solid food, the nanny should record exactly what the child ate at each meal. It is especially important that the nanny pay attention to the child's reactions after meals when new foods are introduced.

-   Did the child seem to like the taste?
-   Did the child enjoy the texture?
-   Did the child have any adverse reactions or allergies such as rash, diarrhea, gas, or constipation?

The nanny could also make notes in the daily logbook providing details on the child's eating habits during the course of the day. Samples of such notes are as follows:

-   The child ate a light breakfast but had a hearty appetite at lunch and dinner.
-   The child ate all of his or her meat at lunch.
-   The child didn't eat much cauliflower at dinner.
-   The child seemed to enjoy the pureed green beans introduced at lunch today.

- The child preferred the pureed butternut squash to the jarred butternut squash.
- The child ate the pieces of cheese but threw all of the peas off the high chair's tray table.

Diapers

Depending on the age of your child, both the parents and nanny may want to record when the baby urinates or has a soiled diaper. Additionally, if there is anything unusual about the child's patterns, then additional notes should be made in the logbook.

Tell your nanny how often to change the child's diaper. Also, instruct her to tell you about any irritations that may have developed. Make sure you have an adequate amount of diaper-rash cream or ointment on hand at all times. If your child has had issues with diaper rashes, then you may want to have a stronger diaper-rash cream or ointment for dealing with rashes, but always ask a medical professional first.

Sleeping

The daily logbook can be used to record the child's sleep routine. Whether or not your child is on a sleep schedule, it is always nice to see how much he or she slept when you were not at home.

One mother was strict about her child's bedtime (seven o'clock) but did not enforce a napping routine. The nanny noticed that the child seemed exhausted after lunch each day, so she started a napping schedule for the child. The child still went down for bed at seven o'clock each evening with the added nap. The mother was delighted because the baby was getting more sleep, and the nap schedule was easy to keep on the weekends when the nanny was not around.

A mother of a premature baby kept a log of her child's eating and sleeping habits on a daily basis and just handed it to the doctor during office visits. When she went back to work, she had her nanny follow the same recordkeeping method in order to track her baby's progress.

In another situation, a mother noticed her toddler son holding his stomach and curling up in a little ball in the corner one afternoon during his usual nap time. When she looked back at the daily logbook that her nanny kept, she realized that he had not had a bowel movement in twenty-four hours; that was unusual for him. She was able to call the doctor and provide all the necessary information relating to eating, sleeping, and bathroom activities in order for her child to be properly diagnosed and treated.

If you notice your nanny does not seem to be very thorough in her recordkeeping, make sure you communicate the importance of keeping consistent notes on a day-to-day basis. Another idea if you don't want to include paperwork in your nanny's tasks is to have the nanny take her own notes during the day and provide an oral recap to you when you return home.

It is also important to stress that the child always comes first. If the child is young, then you may want to tell the nanny to feed your child meals before she eats. If necessary, ask your nanny to eat breakfast at home or to come to your home early and eat breakfast before you have to leave in the morning. Additionally, if your nanny is coming at night, then have her eat dinner before arriving so she can focus on your child, unless she wants to eat when the child goes to sleep.

Question: Do you feel that you have good time-management skills?
Follow-up: Will you be able to keep to my child's schedule?

If the nanny candidate is not wearing a watch when you interview her, you may want to ask how she keeps track of time. Perhaps she uses her mobile phone as her clock—that is completely acceptable. If your child is on a schedule and keeping that routine is important to you, then you need to make sure the nanny understands the importance of keeping an eye on the time.

Keeping track of time will mean something different to a nanny in charge of a baby versus one who watches a school-aged child. However, time-management skills are important for a nanny to possess, no matter the age of the child.

For a younger child, watching the time and knowing when to feed the child a snack or meal is crucial. As the child gets older, the nanny may have to get the child to school or activities in a timely manner. Many schools and after-school programs have strict drop-off and pickup times, so make sure the nanny knows the importance of respecting time limitations or windows. Some summer day camps even charge the family late fees if the child is not picked up on time. Make the nanny aware of these policies that may have financial repercussions. Always stress that safety comes first, of course. But, be sure to communicate any policies regarding time to the nanny so she understands the responsibility and value of keeping track of time.

If you require your nanny to record daily eating, sleeping, or playing times in a logbook, emphasize the importance of making sure the times she records are accurate. One mother of a premature baby told her nanny that it was extremely important to accurately record the feeding times as well as how many ounces of formula or breast milk the baby took at each feeding. The mother needed to show the doctor how the child's health was progressing. Placing a spiral notebook with a pen on a dresser in the baby's room was the perfect way to ensure these feedings were recorded and never lost.

A father discovered that putting his old digital sports watch next to the daily logbook was the ideal way to achieve nearly complete accuracy in terms of recording feeding and sleeping times. That way, both the nanny and the parents were on the same clock.

Question: Will you prepare our child's bottles or food?
Follow-up: Are you comfortable cooking, steaming, or pureeing food for our child?

If nutritious food is important to you, then make it clear to the nanny that she should only feed the child food that you provide. Moreover, she should not bring in food for your child from outside your home without clearing it with you first.

Asking the nanny candidate if she would feel comfortable preparing bottles or food for the child is not out of the ordinary. Many families want to hire a nanny who is capable of doing these food-preparation duties as part of her role in their household. It is important to manage your expectations, though. For instance, do not expect your nanny to prepare a five-course meal for you and your partner. As a matter of fact, you should only expect the nanny to prepare food for your child, not for any adults in your household unless it was agreed upon up front. Also, you must realize that the nanny may only prepare a very basic meal, depending on her comfort level in the kitchen. Remember, the nanny is most likely not a professionally trained chef or culinary expert. Her primary responsibility is taking care of your child.

It is up to you to make food or bottle preparation easy for your nanny. You should make sure that you have all the supplies ready and visible so the nanny can work in a timely and efficient manner. If you would like the nanny to make easy meals for your child or simply puree some fruit or vegetables, you may want to give her recipes or meal plans to keep her organized as well as to accustom her to your family's eating habits.

One mother provided her nanny with index cards that had simple and quick recipes detailing various food purees for her child. The mother steamed vegetables and cut up fruit and put them in labeled containers in the refrigerator. During the child's nap time, the nanny followed the recipes and froze the purees in ice-cube trays. When the mother returned home, she popped the cube purees into freezer bags or containers; labeled the contents; and stored them in her freezer. Here are examples of quick and easy recipes (always check with your child's doctor before introducing new foods and take any allergies into consideration):

Smashed Avocados

- Wash avocados.
- Remove the pits.
- Scoop the inside out into a bowl with a spoon.
- Sprinkle with a dash of lemon to avoid browning, if desired.
- Smash with a fork for chunky consistency, or puree in a blender or food processor for smooth consistency. (Add water only if needed.)
- Serve some of it and freeze the rest in ice-cube trays for another meal.

Zucchini

- Wash zucchini.
- Peel the skin.
- Slice the zucchini into cubes.
- Steam zucchini.
- Puree zucchini in a blender or food processor (usually, you will not have to add water).
- Serve some of it and freeze the rest in ice-cube trays for another meal.

Pears

- Wash pears.
- Peel the skin.
- Remove the core.
- Cut the pear into cubes.
- Either mash with a fork or potato masher or blend until smooth (adding water if needed).
- Serve some of it, and freeze the rest in ice-cube trays for another meal.

One mother admitted she was so worried about her young child's tongue getting burned by food that was served too hot that she served everything directly from the refrigerator or at room temperature. She instructed her nanny to do the same. Specifically, she told her never to use the microwave, stove, or oven to heat her child's food. She knew that her approach may have sounded extreme to many people. But it provided her much-needed peace of mind to know that when she was away from home, she didn't have to worry about her child's tongue getting burned.

Maybe you do not want to go as far as to tell your nanny to never serve warm oatmeal or meatballs, but you should discuss specifics surrounding food preparation (including temperature levels) with your nanny in advance of any feedings. Additionally, you should communicate with your nanny about serving plates or dishes that are microwave or oven safe if heating is required.

You should always ask your nanny for feedback regarding your child's eating habits when he or she is not in your presence. It is good for you to monitor what your child likes or dislikes and how much your child is eating.

One mother told her nanny to feed her child yogurt with lunch every day to increase the child's dairy intake. After several feedings, the child did not seem very interested in the yogurt. The nanny voiced her concern and suggested the mother buy cottage cheese to give the child a little more variety. After one feeding, the child was hooked on cottage cheese. The mother was happy that her nanny not only spoke up but also offered her a healthy, appropriate alternative that the child enjoyed.

Question: Do you feed children inside or outside the home?
Follow-up: Will you abide by our house rules regarding location of the child's meals?

A lot of parents want to develop consistency when it comes to the location of where their children eat their meals. Some parents desire most (if not all) of their children's meals to be eaten inside the home as opposed to allowing their child to "eat on the run" or outside the home. These parents may argue that the child may have a more positive eating experience if he or she is not rushed or distracted by outside elements. Additionally, parents cite the fear that if their child is eating outside the home, he or she may want to eat food from other children or other families that may not be appropriate for their child.

If you prefer your child eats his or her meals in your home, then tell the nanny it is important to you that she abide by this house rule. She may need to have good time-management skills to avoid feeding the child meals outside the home. The nanny may have to feed the child lunch at home before venturing out to a playdate. Let the nanny know that it is neither ideal nor acceptable to feed your child meals at classes, playgrounds, parks, or museums. Specifically, tell your nanny to avoid taking your child into diners, delis, and restaurants so your child will not be tempted by the food choices available and will maintain her or his eating schedule.

Depending on your child's schedule or routine, it may be impossible to avoid eating meals outside the home. If you are more open to where your child eats his or her meals or snacks, then let your nanny know that as well. Some parents encourage their nanny to set up lunch on a picnic table or blanket when the weather is nice outside. You can still control what your child eats, if that is important to you, by discussing what types of food are best eaten outside the home.

One mother who was extremely health conscious was quite shocked when the nanny told her that the child was offered packaged sugary snacks at an extracurricular class. However, the nanny informed the mother that cheese cubes and bananas were also offered as a healthier alternative. The nanny gave the child bananas during the snack break, but the child was not pleased. That afternoon, the nanny told the mother that the child was quite upset that she was not allowed to have the colorful packaged snack that many other children were indulging in right in front of her. The mother reassured the nanny that she had done the right thing by feeding the child the healthier option. Later that evening, after thinking about the situation, the mother went grocery shopping and found some multigrain crackers that closely resembled what the other children were eating. She told her nanny to allow the child to have fruit or vegetables if offered and also to bring the multigrain crackers to the class in case her child wanted something similar to what other children were eating. Additionally, she contacted the class instructor to get approval to bring food from the outside into the classroom for her child. In the end, her child was happy, as was the nanny, who felt comfortable in her communications with the mother.

Question: Will you make sure the child wears either a bib or appropriate clothing at mealtime?

Follow-up: Will you wash or soak any clothing that the child gets dirty, soiled, or stained under your watch?

There is nothing more irritating than seeing marinara sauce painted all over a beautiful white shirt or dress. Make it clear to your nanny that clothing for your child is not disposable, and you believe in getting a lot of mileage out of his or her outfits. However, remember that it is impossible to avoid stains entirely, but with proper planning, you and your nanny can take preventative measures to lessen the chances of ruined outfits.

If you have a toddler, then have plenty of bibs available so the nanny just has to grab one before each feeding. One mother raved about her child's bib because it was almost like a mini-apron that protected her child's clothes. The waterproof bib was stain resistant as well. The nanny just had to wipe it off after each feeding. One bib could last a family several years and be handed down to several children.

For older children, it is important that they do not wear soiled clothing to school or an event. If the older child is eating something that may be a little sticky or messy, it is a good idea to have the nanny suggest that the child wear a T-shirt over his or her outfit or change into the nicer outfit once mealtime is finished.

Additionally, you should always have a stain-removal substance near your sink or washing machine, so if there are any issues with food on clothing, the nanny has the supplies she needs for quick action on the garments. You will want to demonstrate to her how to best deal with stains on your child's clothing so that she is prepared when the time comes. Accidents do happen, so if you have carpeting or rugs, make sure they are protected during mealtime or snacks.

Question: Would you be willing to do certain household chores when the child is napping or at classes?

Follow-up: What types of chores have other families had you do in the past?

You should not assume that the nanny candidate you interview expects to do any more than focus on taking care of your child. However, if you want to expand her role in your household, then ask her up front if she is onboard with taking on additional chores and responsibilities when the child is sleeping, in a class, or at a playdate.

A nanny is not a cleaning person. However, it is perfectly acceptable for you to instruct her to take care of some child-related chores when she has downtime.

Some chores you may want your nanny to do may include the following:

- tidying up the child's play area or room
- washing the child's laundry
- folding the child's laundry
- putting the child's clothes away
- organizing the child's toys
- preparing meals or bottles
- cleaning the child's dishes, utensils, cups, or bottles
- arranging or alphabetizing the child's books
- organizing art supplies
- replenishing your child's diaper bag with supplies
- packing for your child if you are taking a trip

Keep in mind that these ideas are only to be implemented if your child is napping or at classes. You should not give the nanny a long list of chores that you expect her to do every day. You may want to ask the nanny what types of extra duties she took on when she worked with other families in past employment situations. Remember, caring for your child is her top priority as a nanny.

One mother was thrilled when her nanny mentioned to her that she always packed for her previous family's baby and toddler when they were embarking on long-weekend car trips. She even verbally provided an organized packing list that she used each time the family scheduled a trip. A sample of a long-weekend packing list is as follows:

Toddler

- four pairs of underwear
- portable potty and bags
- a few books
- two pairs of pajamas
- three pairs of pants or jeans
- three shirts
- two sweaters or cardigans
- three pairs of socks
- walking shoes
- mittens
- hat
- warm jacket
- bathing suit, cover-ups, goggles, and pool sandals

Baby

- package of diapers, wipes, cream, diaper bag
- teething ring
- a few books
- two pajamas
- three or four onesies
- three pairs of pants
- three shirts
- two sweaters or cardigans
- three pairs of socks

- walking shoes
- mittens
- hat
- warm jacket
- bathing suit, cover-ups, goggles, swim diapers, and pool sandals

Accessories

- portable crib
- umbrella stroller
- twin inflatable mattress for toddler to sleep on floor

Bath accessories for kids

- small travel soap and shampoo
- toothbrushes and toothpaste
- inflatable bathtub
- emergency medicine and thermometer

Food and beverages

- small cooler with ice packs
- sippy cup for toddler—water
- bottle for baby—water
- sippy cup for toddler—milk
- bottle for baby—milk
- bibs
- travel utensils/flatware set
- healthy snacks: yogurt, applesauce, crackers, fruit (pears, peaches, apples), dried cereal

A nanny who is responsible for a school-aged child may have large chunks of free time during the day while the child is in class. During the interview process, ask the nanny candidate if she is receptive to filling her time by handling your grocery shopping, personal errands, light house-keeping, cooking, or other useful tasks. You may find that the nanny loves to create flower arrangements, wrap presents, bake cakes, or inventory clothing. If your child has an upcoming birthday party, perhaps the nanny can organize and fill gift bags for each attendee or make place cards for the seating arrangements. Utilizing the nanny's skills in the best way possible will make everyone happy; she will not be bored in her free time, and you can check off items from your endless to-do list.

Question: Can you clean up food and utensils after meals, clean and sterilize bottles, and tidy up all toys or books at the end of your day?
Follow-up: Would you mind doing the child's laundry on a weekly basis?

It is perfectly acceptable to ask and expect your nanny to clean up anything that was used by or for your child during the day. It is a good idea for your nanny to involve your child in the tidying process as well. You may instruct the nanny to teach your child how to clean up his or her toys, art projects, games, sporting equipment, dress-up clothing, and other playtime items, as children need these skills once they hit school age. Together, your nanny and child can make up clever little songs or rhymes to make the process more enjoyable and less cumbersome.

You should be specific regarding what you expect her to clean up each day. Show your nanny how to use your household appliances. Make sure you tell her where the dishwashing detergent is kept and give her a list of anything you do not want to be put in the dishwasher. If necessary, show your nanny how to use your baby's bottle sterilizer or any other household gadgets that are frequently used with your child.

You can use sticky notes to detail the specific tasks you want accomplished each day as in these examples:

Bottles

- After feedings, wash out the bottles and nipples with the brush provided.
- Sterilize the bottles.
- Dry the sterilized bottles on the bottle-drying rack.

Meals

- After feedings, wash all utensils, plates, and bowls by hand with the brush provided.
- Put all glass containers that held the food in the dishwasher.

- Wipe off or wash the high-chair tray and seat cushion.
- Sweep the floor underneath the high chair.
- Place the used bib in the hamper and take out a new bib for the next meal.

If you have a washer/dryer that is convenient for your nanny to get to, then you may want to ask her to do your child's laundry each week as part of her responsibilities. Do not expect the nanny to do laundry for you or your partner unless that was something you agreed upon in the interview process, as nannies typically take care of the child's belongings only. Many families hire separate cleaning people or housekeepers for the overall household maintenance (deep cleaning, family laundry, and sometimes cooking). Those people are not responsible for serving your childcare needs.

It is important not to expect too much from your nanny. She is not your personal chef, cleaning person, stylist, and concierge. Her number-one priority is the responsibility for and care of your child. If you force too many duties on your nanny, then your child may suffer from lack of attention, and his or her safety may be compromised.

Think about your limitations, and do not expect your nanny to exceed what you can do as one person. Keep in mind that childcare is your nanny's main priority, not picking up your dry cleaning or buying your seasonal gifts. Parents can get carried away with their demands and sometimes need to step back into rational territory to analyze and set sensible and fair expectations of the nanny. Just be careful that what you are asking her to do is reasonable in the allotted time she is with your family each day or week. You do not want your nanny to feel stressed or resentful when taking care of your child. The bottom line is that your child should always come first.

Also, remember that your nanny is not your shrink. She does not need to know intimate details of your personal life. Even if you had a terrible day outside the home, spare her the minutiae. When you return home, try to keep the conversation centered on the child's day. Furthermore, you should discuss items that your nanny wrote down in the nanny's daily logbook. Feel free to ask her about any issues or new milestones.

Question: Are you an organized person?
Follow-up: Would you be willing to help organize our child's schedule, belongings, and supplies?

It is extremely important for your nanny to be organized. Taking care of a child is a huge responsibility and one that should not be taken lightly. When you meet the nanny, ask her if she feels she is an organized person. Ask her to tell you how she keeps organized on a daily basis (planners, notebooks, notes, or other creative methods).

You should tell the nanny candidate that you and your child will depend on her to always be prompt and ready for action. If a nanny candidate shows up to her interview fifteen minutes late, you should ask her if she is habitually tardy for appointments. If you verbally gave the nanny candidate detailed directions to your home and she calls you while on the way to the interview to ask you for directions again, then you may have a problem with her listening or organizational skills.

Your nanny will be responsible for a multitude of agreed-upon tasks while she is caring for your child that may include feedings, activities, naps, baths, and classes. If your child is on a strict eating and sleeping routine, then the nanny must watch the clock throughout the day in order to follow the child's schedule. It is mandatory that your nanny knows how to manage and control her time in order to effectively care for your child.

One mother took organization a step further by asking her nanny to help her organize her child's clothing while the child was at school. The mother bought large plastic containers and asked her nanny to help her neatly fold all of the clothing that the child had outgrown and place them in the containers by size. The nanny also put all coordinating pieces or outfits together, so the mother did not have to match things up if she needed to pull something out of the container. The nanny used brightly colored markers and big white stickers to clearly label the contents of each container. The labels had information on the size and quantity of the clothing items. For example, one container with a label may include the following:

Clothing: Baby Boy
Sizes 6–9 months

- five white long-sleeve onesies
- six printed short-sleeve onesies
- eight footed pajamas
- two blue coordinating jogging sets with pants/jackets
- seven pairs of socks
- two winter hats
- one pair of mittens
- one winter jacket
- one snowsuit

The mother was so happy with her nanny's organizational abilities that she asked her nanny to work on the project on an ongoing basis as the child outgrew clothing items. She even had to go out to buy her nanny more large containers.

When you do hire a nanny, you will want to make sure she has everything she needs to properly care for your child. Also, monitor your child's supplies on a weekly (if not daily) basis. You do not want to be forced to run out to the convenience store at ten o'clock at night in a snowstorm because you ran out of diapers. And you certainly do not want your nanny to panic if she cannot find a necessary item.

It is a good idea to keep the communication lines open with your nanny and ask her to keep a written list of needed supplies. Also, you may want to ask her for her opinion on certain brands or styles of items.

One mother complained to her child's nanny about diapers that leaked every single night. The child often awoke in the middle of the night with wet pajamas and a wet crib sheet. The nanny had four children of her own, not to mention several years of experience in babysitting. She offered a simple suggestion to the mother—try a different brand of diapers in a bigger size that are specifically for overnight use. The mother welcomed the suggestion and promptly purchased the new diapers after work. Both the mother and baby were rewarded as the baby never leaked through a diaper at night again.

Here are some supplies to keep at home (depending on your child's age):

- diapers (daytime and overnight)
- wipes
- diaper-area cream or ointment
- hand sanitizer or disinfectant wipes in every room of your home, especially by the changing table
- blankets for swaddling, tummy time, and so on
- burp cloths
- bibs
- changing pad covers (a few of them in case of accidents)
- beverages as well as bottles/sippy cups and cleaning brushes
- extra crib or bed sheets
- bulb syringe
- child safety products (such as outlet covers, table bumpers, toilet locks, latches for drawers, and so on)
- first-aid kit (adhesive bandages, antiseptic wash/ointment, alcohol rubs)
- brush and comb
- toothbrush and toothpaste
- nail clippers or scissors; nail file
- petroleum jelly/lotion
- sunscreen
- sunglasses
- seasonal accessories (rain boots, umbrellas, snow pants, hats, mittens)
- tissues

- appropriate outerwear (warm jacket in the winter months and rash-guard shirts in the summer months) and shoes (boots in the winter months and water shoes in the summer months)
- bathtub or bath mat
- washcloths/towels
- hypoallergenic lotion, soap, and laundry detergent
- shampoo
- food and utensils
- thermometer
- appropriate medicine for pain or fever reduction (check with the child's doctor)

You should always let the nanny know where you keep your child's car seat in case of emergencies. If the car seat is not installed in a car that she has access to, then show her how to install it in a car or a taxi.

Also, show your nanny how to use your child's stroller. Every stroller is very different, so spend a few minutes and give your nanny a quick tutorial on how to fold it, adjust the angle, and use the parking brake. A few minutes of your time will prove to be extremely helpful to your nanny and potentially lessen her stroller frustrations.

Question: Do you know how to keep children looking neat and well groomed?

Follow-up: Is there anything you do not like to do when it comes to maintenance tasks?

You can tell the nanny up front that helping to groom your child and maintain his or her clean appearance is part of her daily responsibilities. However, you may want to make it clear to her that if there is anything specific that she is uncomfortable doing, she should tell you.

You may want to ask your nanny to assist with some of the following maintenance tasks:

- keeping the child's face and hands clean
- brushing or combing the child's hair
- helping the child brush her or his teeth after every meal as well as flossing in the evening
- clipping or filing the child's fingernails or toenails when needed
- applying sunscreen on the child

Some babies or younger children may intensely dislike grooming activities and may cry to and resist them. Make sure the nanny will be gentle or be willing to learn to use special techniques to reduce the sensitive child's discomfort. Younger children are just learning how to take care of themselves, so most likely they will need supervision and assistance when participating in grooming activities. If the younger child has dry skin or chapped lips, encourage your nanny to teach him or her to apply lotion or ointment to certain areas a few times a day. Your nanny should help the child comb or brush her or his hair in the morning and after physical activities. However, do not expect your nanny to be an expert hair stylist and elaborately style your child's hair. Your nanny does not work at a spa, so do not mandate that she polish your daughter's fingernails or trim your son's hair. Ask your nanny if she is comfortable with filing or cutting your child's nails when necessary (with a child-sized manicure kit, if necessary). If she is not up to the task, then make sure you take care of that maintenance ritual. Also, make it clear that your younger child may need assistance with certain grooming rituals such as brushing teeth after every meal. The nanny can also facilitate the tooth-brushing process by putting toothpaste on the child's toothbrush so it is ready to go.

Older children often need reminders from the nanny even though they can groom themselves. For instance, before they grab food to snack on, the nanny may have to encourage them to wash their hands. Older children may need to take additional steps when taking care of their oral hygiene. That may involve flossing, plaque rinses, or fluoride treatments. Oftentimes, older children need gentle reminders to make sure their hair is presentable when leaving the house for an outside activity.

Nowadays, applying sunscreen protection year round has become an important part of daily skin maintenance in many households, no matter the age of the person. Depending on your doctor's advice, you may want to tell the nanny to apply sunscreen to your child in the morning and to also reapply as needed throughout the day. Some older children like to apply their own sunscreen, but be clear with your nanny that they may need reminders every few hours to put a little extra on to avoid sunburns. If they are going to an outdoor activity or camp, then make sure the nanny leaves sunscreen with them so that your children can protect their skin when they are on their own.

CHAPTER 6

Typical Day: Modeling Your Nanny's Day

● ● ●

As THE PARENT OR GUARDIAN, it is up to you to guide your nanny to make each of your child's days as ideal or near perfect as possible. If you are not united at the beginning, it may be hard to develop unity as time passes.

Question: What do you envision your typical day would be like with my child?

Follow-up: Would you mind incorporating some of my ideas with your ideas so we can work to achieve an ideal day?

After you ask the nanny candidate how she expects to spend a typical day with your child, listen carefully to her response. Allow her the time to expand upon her answers. Do not interrupt her when she is speaking. Although it may be hard for you to stay silent, you want her to talk freely and openly about her style as well as her ideas for your child's day before you add your input.

If you feel as if the nanny cannot answer the question, then maybe she is not as experienced as you need her to be for your childcare situation. If you think the nanny will attempt to do too many activities in one day, then you may need to rein in her enthusiasm. On the flip side, perhaps you believe that the nanny has a good basic framework for your child's day, but she needs help filling in the details. Then assist her in closing the gaps by offering your suggestions.

It is a good idea to direct your nanny with specific activities that you want integrated into your child's daily life. No matter how old the child, when you think about your child's typical day, you may want to have the nanny incorporate some of the following activities:

- **Feeding/snack time:** Have food that you approve of readily available in your home. In order to save time spent on food preparation, you can buy precut fruits, vegetables, and cheeses that your child and nanny can easily grab at any time. If your child likes to assist the nanny in preparing meals or snacks, then have easy-to-do recipe cards on hand for your nanny. Such recipes may include "ants on a log," consisting of celery, peanut butter or sunflower seed butter, and raisins, or "pretend burgers" made up of round crackers, cheese, and lettuce.

- **Classes**: Sign up your nanny and child for classes that they can do together while getting to know each another such as yoga, music, dance, or art. Many museums, zoos, and libraries offer free drop-in classes for members and their childcare providers that are great for children.
- **Creative expression (art projects, crafts, and so on):** Show your nanny the area in your home where you want her and your child to "get messy" and have fun exploring shapes, textures, or materials. If the nanny isn't a natural artist, perhaps you may want to buy some canvases and paints to encourage free painting, purchase beads and elastic for simple jewelry making, or even collect shells for napkin-ring creations.
- **Reading:** Develop the love of learning at an early age. Whether you wish the nanny to read board books or chapter books to your child, make sure you have a good supply of reading materials on hand. If you have older children, perhaps encourage your nanny to take them to the library or a bookstore to pick out a book "just right" for their reading level.
- **Music:** Fill your home with music. Whether you like classical, jazz, show tunes, or kids' classics, you should have music available in rooms that the child and nanny use for playing or eating.
- **Free play:** Organize shelves so your nanny and child can easily pull down toys, games, costumes, and blocks for playtime. Also, if your nanny speaks a foreign language, encourage your nanny to teach your child her native tongue through play or music.
- **Structured play:** Arrange playdates with other children and their caretakers who live in your community. Some parents take pride in their playdate planning skills, while others admit to being lackluster playdate coordinators. Nannies are the same. If you want an outgoing nanny who can organize a busy social calendar for your child, then be up front about that in the interview process. Also, you must realize that you may have to take the step to make introductions between your nanny and the parent or caregiver of your

child's favorite friends and classmates. Many nannies take great pride in their ability to learn the social ropes quickly and navigate the playground benches with great skill. Depending on how strong your nanny's network is, you may be happily surprised to find your child is not only having playdates with his or her friends but also meeting new friends.

If the nanny candidate seems unwilling to incorporate your ideas with hers, then she may not be the right candidate for your family. Remind her that the parent-nanny relationship is a team unit.

Question: How do you think a child should be dressed to go outside in warm weather? How about cold weather?
Follow-up: Will you follow a checklist for dressing our child for the outdoors?

Whether the child is going for a stroller ride to the park or a walk down the street, he or she should be dressed appropriately and comfortably by your nanny. Additionally, for the school-aged child, wearing appropriate attire for the specific day's weather conditions is extremely important. Even if the child's commute to school is short and quick, he or she may have a long outdoor recess period or a field trip, so the child needs to be prepared for being outdoors for extended amounts of time.

It is critical that the nanny pay attention to the weather forecast so she can anticipate any potential changes in the weather patterns during the day and account for those varied conditions. For example, although it may have been a sunny morning when the child left for school, clouds and precipitation may come into play later in the day, and if the child is not prepared for the change in weather, the nanny may have to bring the child appropriate garments and accessories.

Warm/sunny weather attire and accessories may include the following:

- sun hat
- rash-guard shirt
- bathing suit and cover-up
- water shoes
- sunshade for the stroller
- sunscreen
- sunglasses

Cold/snowy weather attire and accessories may include the following:

- hat that covers the child's ears
- mittens or gloves

- scarf or neck warmer
- jacket or coat
- boots
- warm pants or leggings
- snowsuit
- blanket for covering the child in the stroller

Wet/rainy weather attire and accessories may include the following:

- raincoat with hood
- waterproof boots
- child's umbrella
- rain cover for the stroller

Question: How do you feel about taking the child on playdates (both indoors and outdoors)?
Follow-up: Do you know other nannies or families in the area?

You and your partner should have a conversation about playdates before you start interviewing nannies. If you decide that playdates are a good idea for the nanny and child to participate in, then communicate that with the nanny candidates. If you have reservations regarding playdates, then also express your specific concerns to the nanny candidates.

One mother was thrilled to discover that her nanny had strong connections with nannies in the area and was able to arrange playdates with other children in the child's age group on a weekly basis. Eventually, the mother even met some of the parents of the children involved in her child's playgroup and formed friendships.

You will want to think about the following before having other nannies and children over to your home or allowing your nanny and child to enter someone else's home:

- Do you know and trust these families, nannies, or children?
- Are their "house rules" similar to yours?
- Are the homes childproofed and safe?
- Will food be served? (It is important to be careful of allergies or other food sensitivities.)
- Are pets/animals living in the home?

Playdates do not have to be conducted in homes or apartments. Sometimes a change of scenery or location is good for both the nanny as well as the child. Many nannies arrange playdates in locations such as these:

- playgrounds
- parks
- bookstores or libraries (both may host children's events)
- museums (some offer family passes or discounts for children)

- children's gyms
- zoos
- nature trails
- community centers
- toy stores that host children's events (pretend tea parties, arts-and-crafts tables, and so on)
- baseball, soccer, or football fields
- local sporting events
- rock-climbing centers
- home or apartment kitchens (where the children make or decorate edible creations)
- aquariums
- botanical gardens
- pumpkin patches
- berry-picking farms
- kid-friendly restaurants, diners, pizza parlors
- kids' concerts
- circus
- marionette theaters
- sewing studios
- arts-and-crafts studios
- dance centers
- karaoke venues

Before your nanny takes your child to a playground or park, make sure she is aware of any tricks or stunts your child may try if she turns her back. One mother warned her nanny that her child had recently figured out how to open the gate at the entrance of the park and tried to "escape." She told the nanny that the child's behavior was unacceptable and she should definitely watch for and discourage such tricks.

Another mother told her nanny that her child loved to climb up the slides. She mentioned that there had been near collisions with other children in the past. Furthermore, the mother mentioned that the nanny should always keep her eye on the child and try to encourage the child to use the stairs to reach the top of the slide.

If your nanny is taking your child outside on a playdate, she may want to pack a little "emergency kit" in her bag or your child's backpack. No matter the age, something always seems to come up when kids are having fun outside, and she will want to be prepared. The kit may include items such as these:

- your child's emergency contact information sheet (physician or dentist names and phone numbers, allergy or other important health information, and so on)
- hand sanitizer or disinfectant wipes
- compact first-aid kit (adhesive bandages as well as antiseptic wash, ointment, and petroleum jelly)
- sunscreen (small bottle or a stick)
- travel-size tissues (which can also serve as toilet paper or a toilet seat cover at public restrooms)

Question: Are you a creative person?
Follow-up: Will you engage my child in creative projects?

Everyone has limitations, including nannies. You may have an artistic side, but your nanny may struggle with arts-and-craft projects, so if it is important to you, then ask her about her creativity in the interview process.

One mother's part-time nanny was an Ivy League art student who had the child finger-painting before she could walk. At the child's first birthday, the mother proudly and prominently displayed her child's artwork, much to the envy of the other parents.

If you do not employ a trained artist, then ask her if she has an appreciation for art and if she would feel comfortable supervising art projects that you devise. You could develop quick-and-easy art projects for your child and write the instructions down on note cards for the nanny to follow. The supervision could be as simple as asking the nanny to watch the child color in a sketchbook in order to make sure he or she is not eating crayons.

Simple arts-and-crafts projects often brighten up a child's day as well as help her or him learn colors and develop fine motor skills. You should remind the nanny to encourage the child throughout construction of any project and to offer him or her positive feedback upon completion.

You may want to keep these supplies on hand for arts-and-crafts or educational products:

- sketchbooks or paper
- washable or bathtub crayons
- construction paper
- canvas packs
- washable markers
- play dough
- washable glue
- fabric
- ribbons
- glitter

- stickers
- pipe cleaners
- washable finger paint
- washable water colors
- colored chalk
- colored pencils
- children's scissors (to be used with adult supervision)
- coloring books
- cotton balls
- feathers
- toilet paper rolls or paper towel rolls (cardboard centers)
- oil pastels

Question: Would you be willing to take my child to classes that I schedule and pay for?

Follow-up: Will you try to make sure my child is well prepared for the classes?

Ask the nanny if she would like to accompany your child to any classes that you schedule. If possible, in the early days of your nanny's employment with your family, you may want to schedule all such classes close to home. Communicate to your nanny the importance of showing up on time and prepared as there is a cost/financial burden associated with many classes. Also, make it clear to the nanny that these scheduled classes are for the child's development, and it is important to keep the child interested or engaged in the activities or curriculum presented.

You should tell the nanny to make sure that your child is dressed appropriately and comfortably for the activities that may take place during class. If the child is working on messy art projects, it may be a good idea to dress him or her in older clothing topped off with an art apron or smock. Some classes are more physically intense, so the child will want to be dressed in clothing that allows for movement but does not have any zippers, buttons, or embellishments that may get caught on certain gym equipment. Tell the nanny if there is anything special she should wear to class. For instance, some children's centers or gyms require that everyone check in their shoes in a cubicle at the front door, so make sure both the child and nanny wear socks to protect their feet.

Additionally, have the nanny provide you with an overview or report on the class, instructor, and activities. Ask her whether she believed the class to be worth the time and money spent and whether your child seemed interested.

One mother was surprised when her nanny returned from a class and told her the instructor was not ideal. She did not think he had much interest or experience in dealing with children. The nanny thought that the environment was rather tense as opposed to relaxed and joyful. The nanny suggested she try a different class with the child on a free-trial basis. The mother respected the nanny's opinion and enrolled the child in another class with a different instructor.

There are so many classes for children that it is often difficult to decide what class to sign your child up for each season. Ask your neighbors and friends for suggestions regarding classes that their children may have taken in your area. Examples of children's classes include the following:

- music
- art
- gymnastics
- sign language
- foreign languages
- dance/movement
- cooking
- soccer, T-ball, or other team sports
- martial arts (tae kwon do, karate)
- religion
- drama
- yoga
- swimming
- rock climbing
- computers or robotics
- writing

If you want your child to have variety, some organizations offer combination classes such as these:

- art with music
- foreign language with cooking
- gymnastics with dance

You should ask your nanny if she is comfortable with the specific class before you sign up your child. For instance, if your nanny is not comfortable in the water, then do not sign your child up for a swimming class that requires the nanny to participate with your child in the pool. Unless you can get a private instructor for your child, save the swimming classes for a day that you or your partner can attend.

Be smart regarding what times you are scheduling your child's classes. For instance, do not schedule a class during naptime or mealtime. If the class is active, make sure your child will have the proper amount of time to digest his or her meal before partaking in the class.

Do not overschedule your child. Most likely, you will have your child home for at least eighteen years, so do not try to pack eighteen years of classes in one year.

Question: Would you feel comfortable taking my child to a doctor's appointment?
Follow-up: Can you ask the doctor any questions I have and communicate the answers back to me?

You should make every effort to be at your child's scheduled doctor's appointments, especially in the early years. However, it is not always practical to participate in every single appointment with your child, so ask the nanny if she is willing to take your child to doctor's appointments and report the details back to you. If possible, it is always best if you try to meet the nanny and your child at the doctor's office, so you can participate in the appointment.

Before you send your nanny to the doctor's office with your child, find out the policy that your physician's office has regarding nonlegal guardians (such as nannies) taking the child to office visits or doctor's appointments. If you must provide a note, then write or type the note ahead of time and give it to your nanny to present upon entering the office. Make sure you provide your signature on the note.

If you have any concerns regarding your child's health or development, then you should provide a list of questions that your nanny can ask the doctor to address these concerns. You should have your nanny take notes and tell you all of the doctor's responses in addition to any new or additional information that may have come out of the office visit.

If vaccinations were administered by health professionals at the child's appointment, whether or not you were present, ask the nanny how the child responded after you left. The following questions may be helpful:

-   Did the child cry? If so, for how long?
-   How did the child react the rest of the day?
-   Did the child sleep longer after the shots?
-   Did you notice any rashes?
-   Does the child seem sore?

Most physicians provide parents with a personal record book to keep track of the child's medical appointments, vaccinations, and height and weight. You should make sure your nanny takes this book with her to the child's appointment and has the doctor or nurse fill out the important details.

Also, ask the nanny when the next appointment should be scheduled in order for you and your child to get an ideal time slot before the practice gets booked.

Question: Would you make sure my child does homework in a quiet place?
Follow-up: Would you be able to supervise my child with homework?

If you desire a nanny that can also serve as your child's tutor, then you will want to let that be known up front. Additionally, when you conduct your nanny search, you may want to find a nanny with particular interest or expertise in subjects such as the following:

- math
- reading
- English
- specific foreign languages
- science
- social studies
- geography
- history
- computers

In one household, English was not the primary language of either working parent. However, the parents wanted the child to not only learn their native tongue but also to have a flawless comprehension of the English language. So they conducted a nanny search with the specific goal of finding an English tutor for the child. After many rounds of interviews, they found the ideal nanny, who helped the child learn and master both spoken and written English.

Please keep in mind that even if someone has advanced degrees, it does not always guarantee that they are patient teachers to children. You will want to watch how the nanny candidate interacts with your child in order to evaluate her teaching or tutoring style. The ideal candidate will make learning a fun, creative, and entertaining experience for your child. You want to hire the candidate who kindly encourages and constructively corrects your child as opposed to the candidate who may know all the answers but cannot communicate effectively.

Some nannies do not have formal educational backgrounds but are avid readers who are extremely knowledgeable about many topics and subject matters. If your nanny has the desire to teach your child the basics, then you should definitely encourage her to help your child with early learning skills by supplying her with important tools such as these:

- flash cards (shapes, letters, numbers, objects, and colors)
- alphabet books, counting books
- learning CDs or DVDs
- place mats with math facts (addition, subtraction, multiplication, and division)
- educational board games (including trivia and maps)
- foreign language cards or bingo games

Some families only need their nannies to make sure their children complete their homework before they come home from work. A nanny does not necessarily need an advanced degree to supervise your child with their homework. You may want her to create a calm, quiet environment for your child to study in and complete assignments without distraction. Also, the nanny could help provide the child with healthy snacks for study breaks in addition to emotional support during more complex or lengthy assignments.

Question: Have you ever taken care of a child with developmental issues or special needs?

Follow-up: Would you feel comfortable taking my child to therapy or special classes as well as doing daily exercises recommended by the experts with the child?

If you have a child with special needs, behavioral issues, or health concerns, you should communicate that to the nanny candidate in the initial conversation. Ask her directly if she is comfortable taking care of a child with certain needs. If she is at all hesitant or expresses concern about her abilities, then she may not be the right fit for your child, so move on to the next candidate.

Depending on your child's situation, you may want to focus on hiring a nanny with experience in dealing with children with special needs and preferably someone who has taken care of a child with similar issues to yours (realizing that all children are unique). A nanny with a medical background may be the ideal hire for your family, but that may not be possible or even necessary. Parents of a special-needs child will want to use extra due diligence to find a nanny who could appropriately care for their child with patience and compassion.

You may want to investigate whether or not the nanny candidate feels comfortable among professionals who may play important roles in the child's life. Depending on the child's specific needs, he or she may be in regular contact with speech therapists, occupational therapists, physical therapists, psychologists, nutritionists, teacher aides, and various doctors or medical professionals.

One mother was pleasantly surprised with her nanny's responses to her child who had physical challenges. Although the nanny was not a trained therapist herself, she understood the importance of early intervention and actively engaged the child in daily exercises that she learned from the parents and therapists. The nanny also brought the child to therapy sessions and verbally provided the parents with detailed progress reports. The nanny developed fun playtime activities that helped the child with her development such as scooping sand into buckets with shovels in the sandbox at the playground and creating structures out of large blocks at home.

Question: Do you have experience taking care of older children?
Follow-up: Are you comfortable with taking older children to school and various activities in addition to supervising them in our home?

I am sure you can remember a time in adolescence when you challenged parental authority, thus showing your desire for independence. The age when parents feel comfortable leaving a child alone is quite personal and varies on a family-to-family basis. It not only depends on the maturity level of the child but also on the environment the child is growing up in. However, some parents with older children feel they need the security of a childcare provider to help them during after-school hours. Those parents who work may need a full-time childcare provider to help the child get off to school in a timely manner and to be there for any school closings, holidays, vacations, or schedule changes.

As you analyze your childcare needs for older children, please ask yourself the following questions:

- Can my child get to school with us or by himself/herself?
- Would a chaperone be a great asset to our household?
- What is our family plan for school closures (scheduled holidays and vacations as well as unscheduled snow days, illnesses, or other surprise issues)?
- Does my child go directly to after-school activities that he or she can walk to, or is a helper needed to get him or her safely from one place to another?
- Does my child need help or encouragement with completing homework assignments, or is my child self-sufficient?
- Could my older child benefit from having a buddy or a mentor?

Some parents hire a nanny or sitter for older children just to give their children companionship and themselves piece of mind. Because a nanny to an older child does not have to be burdened with diaper changes, feedings, or tummy time, parents may want to consider hiring someone the child respects yet can view as a friendly authority figure. Parents should clearly define the nanny's roles and perhaps even discuss nanny responsibilities with the older child so that everyone is on the same page. Together, the parent and child could come up with a road map detailing how the nanny's hours are spent. This way, the older child feels a sense of independence for acting as a critical member of the nanny selection process and may not be as resistant to an extra household helper.

Some nanny's responsibilities you may want to consider and evaluate when interviewing a nanny for your older child are listed below.

Homework Help

- Is the nanny willing and able to monitor the child's completion of his/her homework each day/night?
- Will the nanny teach the child good homework habits? Here are examples of habits to teach:
  1. Completing assignments in a quiet place without distractions like phones or electronic devices
  2. Focusing on the task at hand with short study breaks (complete with healthy snacks) when needed
  3. Managing stress when solutions do not come easily
- Can the nanny review the child's work for errors or suggestions?
- Can the nanny quiz the child for upcoming tests?

After-School Transporting

- Will the nanny be able to get the child to and from school and extracurricular activities in a safe and timely manner?
- Does the nanny drive?
- Is the nanny comfortable using various means of public transportation with your child (buses, trains, subways, ferries, and so on)?
- Is the nanny willing to walk with your child to and from school or activities?
- Does the nanny know the geographic area you live in well?

- Can the nanny follow street directions accurately?
- Will the nanny ensure your child gets to his or her destinations safely and on time?

Other Chores

- While the child is at school or busy with an activity, will the nanny tackle household chores such as light cleaning, dusting, vacuuming, and laundry?
- If the child selected some quick, easy, and healthy recipes, would the nanny be able to make them for lunch or dinner?
- If you provide the funding, will the nanny run household errands such as picking up the family's laundry at the dry cleaners, returning library books, dropping off packages at the post office, selecting birthday gifts, or picking up groceries while the child is not at home?

Creative Activities

- Does the nanny have ideas of creative activities to engage the child in when there is a lull in the schedule, including exposing him or her to something new? (Examples include knitting/crocheting, cooking, playing music, making art projects, visiting museums, building models, and so on.)

Parents may want to purchase inexpensive and easy craft projects or a craft idea book to keep in the home for the nanny and child to do together.

Extracurricular Activities

- Can the nanny keep the child off of electronic devices by encouraging him or her to read, play a board or card game, or engage in a healthy physical activity?
- Will the nanny engage in sports with the child?

Sports were very important for one family. The parents targeted their nanny search to find a caretaker who was nurturing and athletic. They succeeded and found an ideal nanny with great athletic abilities, and as a result, their little ones were the talk of the tennis court.

Question: Will you monitor our older child's interactions with peers?
Follow-up: Will you give us feedback on anything that seems interesting, suspicious, or unsettling about our child or his or her classmates?

It is one thing to be with a child physically, but it is another thing to be truly mentally and emotionally present when one is with a child.

Your nanny should have her eyes and ears open to the interactions and conversations that take place in front of her when your child is with peers, whether in your home, in a car, at an activity, or walking home from school or an event. If your nanny sees or hears something that seems troublesome, such as negative talk, peer pressure, foul language, or other inappropriate behavior, she should report back to you or your partner immediately. Of course, you should also encourage your nanny to give you reports that show your child in a positive light.

For example, if a nanny overheard a conversation between two tween girls about seeing a classmate throw up in the bathroom after lunch, she should tell a parent. The parent could use the information as a teachable moment and address the issue of eating disorders so that the child understood the health risks of his or her peer's actions. Additionally, the parent could alert the troubled student's teacher, parent, or guardian about the child's dangerous behavior.

If a nanny overhears the child talking rudely to a peer (or vice versa), she should also inform the parent, who could investigate and figure out what is causing the negative reactions. Conversations involving unsupervised parties or events should also be communicated to the parent. The nanny should feel comfortable enough to tell you if she believes your child or his or her friends are engaging in harmful activities.

Childhood is about building self-esteem and learning how to interact in our greater society, so any feedback that the nanny can give you about your child's behavior or interaction with others is important to his or her development.

CHAPTER 7

Safety and Pets: An Extra Level of Protection

● ● ●

JUST AS YOUR CHILD WILL take her first step, eat her first banana, and speak her first word, she will have her first accident at some point. Arm your nanny with everything she needs to make sure your child is well cared for when this happens.

Question: Do you have any formal training or certifications in childcare?
Follow-up: Please provide an example of an emergency situation and how you handled it.

Some local doctor's offices, hospitals, or community groups offer classes in childcare, child safety, first aid, or CPR on a regular basis. If the nanny candidate lacks formal training, you should ask her up front if she would attend a class or session and offer to pay her tuition.

If the nanny candidate took childcare, child safety, first aid, or CPR training a long time ago, then ask her if she would be willing to take a refresher course. Tell her that you would be happy to sign her up and compensate her for any fees. Let her know that the class could be taken at a time that would work with her schedule. Be clear that you value safety. Make sure she realizes that refresher classes are a great way to reinforce information and techniques that she might have previously learned. Moreover, you or your partner may also want to attend a class with her to update your skills.

Asking the nanny candidate a situational question regarding how she dealt with an emergency situation tests her ability to handle situations under pressure.

Make sure that you communicate your family's safety rules to your nanny. These safety rules may include the following:

- Call 911 if the child is in danger.
- Call Poison Control at 1-800-222-1222.
- Do not leave the child unattended (whether inside or outside).
- Never leave the child alone on the changing table, sofa, or bed.
- Keep the child away from the oven, stove, windows, water (faucets, toilet, sinks), and electrical outlets.
- Keep the child away from water sources such as pools, lakes, rivers, ponds, creeks, streams, or the ocean.
- Do not leave small objects around the child (potential choking hazards).

- Keep the home entrance doors locked.
- Do not give the child medicine or vitamins unless cleared by parents.
- Do not let the child answer the door.
- Do not let the child answer the telephone.
- Do not allow the child to leave the home without adult supervision.
- Always hold hands with the child and look both ways when crossing a street.
- Make sure the child always wears a helmet when riding a bike or scooter.
- Do not talk to strangers when you are with a child.
- Never light candles (keep matches up high in a cupboard).
- Keep all personal information private (online and off-line).
- Always ask for help if you need it.

One mother told her nanny not to give her child any medicine without asking her permission. One evening, she looked in the laundry bag and noticed that her child's pajamas were stained with liquid medicine. The child had had a slight fever earlier that day, but the mother had not authorized the nanny to administer medicine to the child. She immediately confronted the nanny, who initially denied giving it to the child but then admitted the act. The mother realized the trust was broken.

Remember to always keep your cell phone on and instruct the nanny to do the same if she has one. Some parents mandate their nanny keep a cell phone, and they are more than happy to set her up with a phone and pay for the monthly bill. Make sure the communication lines are always open between you and your nanny. Raising and caring for your child is a team effort. Safety should always come first.

Question: Will you make sure my child is supervised by you at all times?
Follow-up: Will you always be near my child when he or she uses technology?

Children of all ages need adult supervision, and that is what you are paying a nanny for each day. Tell the nanny that it is unacceptable for her to leave your child unsupervised or in the care of someone else unless prearranged by you. One quick lapse of judgment may result in harmful consequences.

It may be tempting for your nanny to leave your young child at the bottom of a staircase to get something at the top of the stairs. However, the child may try to follow the nanny and fall down the stairs. Accidents happen within seconds. Children can be very quick. The nanny needs to exercise good judgment and make sure she watches your child at all times.

Also, tell the nanny it is inappropriate to leave your child alone with someone she knows (a friend, a relative, or another nanny) unless she asks your permission in advance. Even though she is comfortable with someone watching your child, you may not be at ease with such a situation. Remind her that you spent a great deal of time finding someone you trusted to care for your child and that you may not have the time to review her "backups."

Additionally, explain to your nanny that you are paying her to care for your child. You are not paying her to run personal errands. If she needs to catch up on errands or appointments, tell her to ask you for a day off in advance so you can arrange alternate care.

One mother had to confront her nanny after coming home every other day and seeing shopping bags by the front door. The child told the mother that the nanny always dragged her to the drugstore after school instead of taking her right home to eat lunch. The mother made it clear that the nanny was free to do any personal shopping when she left work in the evening.

It is also important to note that if you have an older child, you will want to communicate to the nanny the importance of supervising all online or Internet communications. If the older child has to finish a homework assignment, the nanny should carefully monitor the child's progress and make sure he or she does not veer to an unsafe or inappropriate website.

Internet safety tips may include the following:

- Never share personal information (the child should not share his or her name, age, address, phone number, e-mail, pictures, gender, or school online).
- Do not share passwords.
- Do not click on pop-ups (especially inappropriate messages, pictures, and advertisements).
- Understand that once something is posted online it will not go away (including comments, pictures, and so on). So it is important to resist the temptation of posting online as things may come back to haunt the child (innocent or not).
- Know that not everything one reads online is true.
- Realize that when in doubt or danger in an online capacity, the child should always ask an adult for assistance.
- Be respectful online, and be mindful of cyberbullying and gossip.
- Never arrange to meet online "friends" in person, as the child could be put in a highly dangerous situation.

Your nanny should also realize that the Internet is a powerful tool, and she should never post pictures, messages, or comments about your family online. Communicate that you want her to respect your family's privacy and not mix your family's personal business with her social media interests.

Obviously, there are many advantages of the Internet, but it is important to teach your child and remind your nanny to avoid the pitfalls. If your family is comfortable with the nanny and child using the Internet together, perhaps suggest they work on a long-term project that the whole family can enjoy. One idea is to have them take digital pictures of the child's old art projects and create a photo album of the artwork that can be printed and ordered as a keepsake.

Question: Have your prior families allowed you to bring visitors to their homes?

Follow-up: Who have you brought into their homes?

Most parents cringe at the thought of their nanny inviting people in her life especially significant others—over to their homes. Visions of the couple making out on the couch while the child is ignored may run through parents' heads.

You should be clear that taking care of the child is the nanny's primary responsibility, and she is paid accordingly for that job. If you do not want any or certain visitors over, then make that a house rule and communicate it to her. Think of the pros and cons relating to visitors such as the following:

- Significant other: helpful or distracting?
- Another nanny friend: valuable or detracting?
- Another child (the nanny's own or another one she takes care of): fun or disruptive?

Please note that if another person comes into your home, you should be aware of all allergies, sensitivities, or health issues. Also, make sure your home is childproofed as appropriate if a child visits.

You should not expect your nanny to receive maintenance or service people into your home when she is alone with your child. Schedule these visits during a time when at least one parent is home. Even though mechanical systems and appliances in your home may break down from time to time and service visits may be hard to schedule, do not expect your nanny to receive repair people when you are not at home. It is unfair of you and too much to ask of the nanny to supervise both the child and the adult service person.

Question: Will you contact me immediately if my child is badly hurt/injured?
Follow-up: Will you inform me of any accidents that happen involving my child when I am not at home?

Accidents will happen. It is unrealistic to believe that your child will go through life without a blemish. You want to gain insight into the nanny's ability to recognize and deal appropriately with a serious injury versus a less serious one. You should let your nanny know that it is important that she informs you of any accidents your child might have had during the day (serious or not). Make sure she tells you about any of the following:

-   head injuries
-   burns
-   scrapes
-   bruises
-   cuts
-   bumps
-   falls
-   spills
-   slips
-   gashes

Also, keep track of the frequency of your child's accidents. You need to make sure the nanny is properly watching your child.

Stress the importance of communicating the specifics surrounding any accidents that occurred when you were not present. If the child hit her or his head, ask the nanny for the exact details of the event as well as the time it occurred. A child who fell off the monkey bars at the playground may have masked his or her initial pain in order to stay longer to play with friends. However, the child's pain could increase as time goes by.

You should make sure the nanny understands that it is critical to step away from an activity and evaluate the child right when an accident happens. If there is a judgment call to be made whether or not the child gets checked out at the hospital for an injury, the nanny should notify you or your child's doctor immediately. Sometimes, it is better for the child's healing process for the nanny to proceed with a doctor's recommendation to take the child to the emergency room of a hospital to get a few stitches rather than treat the injury with a bandage at home.

Question: Do you have pets of your own?
Follow-up: Are you comfortable around pets? Please let us know which household animals you are not comfortable with.

If you have pets, make sure the nanny candidate is comfortable with your animals right away. Ask her if she has any allergies to certain animals. Do not expect your nanny to load up on allergy medicine before she comes to your home each day because she is allergic to your cat.

If you do not have pets but would consider getting some in the future, check to see whether the nanny candidate is comfortable with the pets you have in mind. If you are an animal lover, then you do not want the nanny to be uncomfortable with pets in your home or around your child.

Some household pets may include:

- fish
- dogs
- cats
- birds
- hamsters
- gerbils
- guinea pigs
- turtles
- snakes
- newts
- lizards

Also, do not mandate that your nanny clean up after your animals or feed them. Unless prearranged, your nanny should not be expected to help with the following chores:

- cleaning aquariums or cages
- feeding animals
- walking dogs

- grooming animals
- picking up animal waste
- shopping for pet food

One mother thought she had found the perfect nanny until the nanny told her she was terrified of dogs. In particular, the nanny was terribly afraid of large dogs. Because the family had a large German Shepherd that they were not willing to part with, the mother knew that nanny candidate was not right for her family but found a nanny who was ideal.

Question: How do you feel about children petting animals that do not belong to them?
Follow-up: Will you make sure the child is protected around all animals?

Whether you are an animal lover or not, if you are not familiar with a particular animal, you may not want your child to get too close to that animal. Your child may be amused by the fluffy white cat that appears on your doorstep or the big black dog that is next to his or her stroller in the elevator. However, if you do not know the animal's temperament, then you and your nanny should keep the child away from it.

A child may innocently tug on an animal's tail out of curiosity only to be bitten by the aggravated animal. The child may even have to make a hospital visit as a result of a few minutes of fun gone wrong. You do not want your child or your nanny to experience panic if you can avoid the situation in the first place.

Animals can be unpredictable, so taking a cautious stance when children are around is not a bad idea. If your nanny thinks you are being too overprotective by not allowing your child to pet animals, then explain to her the many unknowns that cause you to be concerned. If you are unfamiliar with the animal, think about the following questions:

- Does the animal have all of its shots?
- Is the animal aggressive or agitated?
- Has the animal been neglected or abused?
- Is the animal hungry?

The day before a planned family vacation, a little boy wandered into an adjacent yard in his neighborhood after he heard a dog barking. The inquisitive boy approached the dog and was bit in the face. It was not the nanny who was watching the boy but his parents who subsequently took the boy to the hospital for treatment. Unfortunately, the parents canceled their family vacation as the boy needed to stay in the immediate area to undergo further treatment and tests in the days that followed the incident.

It is usually a good idea to tell your nanny to keep your child away from cages with animals. No matter how big or small the animal, you never know how the animal will react if the child gets too close to the cage. Never allow the child to put any part of his or her body near a cage. Instruct the nanny to demonstrate good judgment if the child wants to feed an animal. For example, dropping a small amount of food into a goldfish bowl may be quite different from feeding a piranha.

CHAPTER 8

Situational Questions:
360 Degrees of Insight

● ● ●

EVERY SITUATION IS DIFFERENT, BUT a series of questions that delve into important issues can reveal valuable insights about your nanny prospect. These situational questions are aimed at better understanding the nanny's childcare experience.

Question: What position should an infant be in when sleeping in a crib?
Follow-up: Will you keep unnecessary objects out of the baby's crib?

This question tests how well the nanny candidate knows her crib safety rules. Many sources agree that it is best if an infant sleeps on his or her back in a crib to reduce the risk of SIDS (sudden infant death syndrome) as well as other sleep-related deaths. However, if your baby has a certain medical condition or if you have a concern, always ask your baby's doctor what is best for your child.

You will want to make sure the nanny knows how to put the baby into the crib on his or her back. Tell her to not be afraid of waking the baby up. She should realize that crib safety is extremely important to your family.

Also, tell her not to place any unnecessary objects such as pillows, blankets, quilts, comforters, loose sheets, stuffed animals, or toys in the baby's crib. Your nanny may question why you do not have bumper pads to coordinate with the baby's window treatments. Explain to your nanny that you are not using bumpers as a safety measure.

Your nanny could be concerned that your baby will get cold without a blanket. Tell her to put proper pajamas or a one-piece sleep sack or wearable blanket (that meets safety standards) on the baby if she thinks temperature is a concern. However, it is important that the baby does not get overheated.

If your nanny believes your baby needs to cuddle up with a stuffed animal in order to get to sleep, tell her that you do not want plush animals in your baby's crib. Let her know that your child is free to play with stuffed animals with her supervision outside the crib, but you do not want to get into the habit of having your child sleep with stuffed animals due to safety precautions.

Question: What temperature do you believe a baby's room should be at? **Follow-up:** Would you please help us maintain a certain temperature in the baby's room?

Different sources will provide you with a variety of opinions relating to the ideal temperature for a baby's room (most seem to say between 65 and 70 degrees Fahrenheit, depending on several factors). Some professionals even advise parents to keep the baby's room warmer during the day and cooler at night. It is best to ask your child's doctor what he or she believes the ideal temperature is for your baby's room.

Once you and your partner (or your medical professional) have decided on an ideal temperature for the baby's room, communicate that to your nanny. Be sure to tell her if the daytime and nighttime temperatures should vary. Additionally, have a room thermometer or baby monitor with temperature control in all of the rooms you expect the baby to frequent, so you can accurately monitor any temperature changes.

Depending on where you live, your nanny may have to battle the heater, air conditioner, room fans, and windows (with proper security bars installed, of course) in order to make the child comfortable. Before you leave your nanny and child at home alone, make sure the room temperature is adjusted appropriately and show your nanny how to make further adjustments. You do not want your child to be too hot or too cold. As a safety precaution, tell the nanny to keep the baby (whether awake or asleep) away from direct contact with sunlight, windows, and fans.

Question: Have you ever experienced a time when a child was crying for an extended period?
Follow-up: How did you handle the crying child?

You should get an idea of how the nanny deals with a difficult and realistic situation involving a crying child. Carefully listen to her response and take note of the following:

- Did she react quickly?
- Did her actions make sense?
- Did she seem patient and caring or frustrated and annoyed?
- Did she know whom to call or contact?

As any parent knows, every day with a child is different, and things do not always go as planned. It is important to discuss your child's disposition with your newly hired nanny. As she spends more time alone with your child, she will learn how your child reacts to certain situations.

One working mother described a time when her normally happy baby cried for over fifteen minutes one day after the nanny fed her lunch. The nanny held and rocked the little girl, but the crying continued. Then the nanny realized that the child's forehead seemed a bit warm. At the half-hour point, she called the mother at work and explained the unusual pattern of crying. The concerned mother promptly left work, came home, and took the baby to the doctor. Apparently, the child was sick, and the nanny's quick thinking enabled the child to get care that afternoon instead of having to wait for an appointment the following day.

Not only do babies cry, but so do older children. If a school-aged child appears sad after school, playdates, or other activities, the nanny should immediately communicate that to the parents so that the problem or situation can be properly investigated.

Question: What are your techniques for disciplining a child?
Follow-up: How do you feel about spanking?

You and your partner should discuss at length and agree upon a set and consistent approach to disciplining your child before talking to nanny candidates. Your disciplinary techniques and measures may evolve over time or as the child grows. However, you should make sure to communicate your beliefs regarding discipline to your nanny. It is important that all of the authority figures or caretakers in your child's life are consistent in their methods of discipline. You want your nanny to be nurturing yet firm when your child does something that needs to be addressed.

Be specific when discussing how your family disciplines the child. For example, if you use the "time-out" approach, you should clarify to the nanny where you want the child placed (a certain chair, a beanbag, or a crib or bed) as well as the duration of the time out (in minutes). If your approach to discipline is to use logical consequences, then if the child fights with a peer over a toy, you should tell the nanny to take the toy away for a set amount of time. Or, if the child knocks down a friend's block structure, the nanny may want to tell him or her to apologize, and then the child should help the friend reconstruct it. You will want to be extremely clear in detailing exactly how you want the nanny to discipline your child.

Also, talk to your nanny about any disciplinary methods that you do not believe in or that you do not want to be used in your home. For example, if you and your partner do not believe a child should ever be spanked, make sure the nanny knows that it is unacceptable to ever spank your child. Washing a child's mouth out with soap after he or she says something inappropriate is another example of a more controversial disciplinary method that you may not believe to be appropriate in your household. Let your nanny know about any other methods of discipline that you do not approve of that should never be used with your child.

Ask the nanny what techniques she uses to discipline a child. Perhaps she can offer creative solutions that you may not have thought of trying with your child.

One mother was surprised when the nanny candidate told her that she tried to use productive methods of discipline with children. When pressed to discuss what she meant by her statement, the nanny explained that she would tell children in a firm voice not to do whatever they had done again and would then redirect their energy to a more constructive task such as making their bed, organizing their toys, or picking up leaves outside. The mother had never thought about this form of discipline, but she decided it just might work for her child.

Question: Have you ever experienced a time when a child had a temper tantrum?

Follow-up: How do you handle an irritable child?

You want to get an idea of how the nanny deals with a child who may be a bit out of control from time to time. When the nanny answers your question, think about the following:

- Was the nanny rational in her actions?
- Did the nanny focus on the child?
- Did the nanny teach the child or purely give up?
- Did the nanny act in a positive or negative way?

There are various ways to deal with temper tantrums, so you will want to hear exactly how the nanny deals with those situations and why she takes certain actions. You may even learn something from her that you can use in the future. Or you may not agree with how she reacted in the past, and you should communicate that to her in a productive manner. The biggest thing you are looking for is an answer that shows the nanny understands that children will have temper tantrums and that she reacts in a way that does not highlight frustration.

One of the easiest ways many people deal with a child's temper tantrum is to remove the child from his or her environment. For example, if the nanny and child are in the grocery store and the child starts loudly complaining (or begins to get physical), tell your nanny it is OK for her to take the child out of the store and head home. It is more important to tend to the child than to worry about grabbing those extra bananas.

Question: Have you ever helped potty train a child?
Follow-up: What successful potty-training techniques have you used for small children?

Depending on the age of your child, your nanny may or may not play an important role in potty training.

Once again, you and your partner must give the nanny clear instructions detailing when and how you want to proceed with potty training the child. In addition, you should provide all the necessary potty-training supplies, which may include the following:

- potty-training seats or seat covers
- a step stool
- potty chairs
- wipes
- several pairs of pull-ups or training pants
- several pairs of underwear
- extra bedsheets or crib sheets for accidents
- any necessary cleaning supplies
- potty-training books for the child
- potty-training dolls for the child
- potty-training rewards (such as charts, stickers, or targets for the toilet)

All adults involved in potty training your child should make potty training a fun experience, not a stressful endeavor for your child. Communicate with the nanny that accidents will happen. You want her to reassure your child that accidents are perfectly acceptable, and it is just a part of the learning process that everyone goes through. Tell the nanny to use a lot of positive reinforcement and encouragement throughout the potty-training process. Your nanny should never punish the child for accidents. You and the nanny should aim to keep the experience positive by introducing children's books about potty training to your child.

If you or your nanny has a creative edge, it is a nice idea to make a fun and colorful potty-training milestone chart with your child. Using colored cardboard or construction paper, you could create a grid chart to detail the child's potty-training progress. The child can stick his or her favorite stickers onto the chart when he or she is successful. An example of a basic potty-training chart is on the following page.

One working East Coast parent was thrilled to discover her nanny's interest and patience in potty training her young son. One day, after a discussion regarding potty training with the mother, the nanny took the child to a children's clothing store and told him to select a packet of his own big-boy underwear. Then, with the parent's permission, the nanny hosted a "potty-training party" at the family's apartment. She invited a few other nannies and children from their playground to the party. Over snacks, he proudly showed everyone his big-boy underwear. The nanny was able to potty train the little boy in no time by making the experience both positive and fun for him.

Basic Potty-Training Chart

(Decorate the chart and use stickers to reward the child's progress.)

	Sunday	Monday	Tuesday	Wednesday	Thursday	Friday	Saturday
1:00 AM							
2:00 AM							
3:00 AM							
4:00 AM							
5:00 AM							
6:00 AM							
7:00 AM							
8:00 AM							
9:00 AM							
10:00 AM							
11:00 AM							
12 NOON							
1:00 PM							
2:00 PM							
3:00 PM							
4:00 PM							
5:00 PM							
6:00 PM							
7:00 PM							
8:00 PM							
9:00 PM							
10:00 PM							
11:00 PM							
12 MIDNIGHT							

CHAPTER 9

Final Question: Final Answer

● ● ●

PUT THE BALL IN THE nanny's court by allowing her to ask you questions.

Question: Do you have any questions for us?
Follow-up: Are you interested in working for our family?

These questions will let you know if the nanny candidate is interested in working for your family.

Please keep in mind that many nanny candidates have not worked in professional office settings. Do not expect the nanny candidate to open up a leather portfolio, pull out a fancy pen, and proceed to read off a long list of questions she typed up in preparation for the interview. However, the nanny candidate should have a few questions that will enable you to assess how serious she is about the job.

Although it seems quite direct to ask the nanny candidate if she is interested in working for your family, it is a way to put her on the spot and get her gut reaction. You may have thought the interview went well, but the nanny may disclose otherwise. Perhaps she has a few pending job offers that she wants you to know about. Maybe she desires to work with children who are different ages or genders than your own. Or the candidate may feel that your family is just not the right fit for her and may want to explore a different working environment.

On a positive note, the candidate may communicate to you that she does see working with your family as a nice arrangement for her. Whatever the answer, you will want to know what your next steps should be—whether you move on to interview the next nanny candidate or start calling her references.

Comprehensive List of Questions

● ● ●

Chapter One Background: Check Closet and Set Course
1. Question: How long have you been a nanny?
Follow-up: Where do you see yourself in the future?

2. Question: How many children have you taken care of at once in one family?
Follow-up: How many children would you ideally like to care for at once?

3. Question: How long-term of a job are you looking for right now?
Follow-up: Will you try to give us advance notice if you need to leave the job with our family?

4. Question: Can I please have a list of names and phone numbers in order to check your references?
Follow-up: Why did each of your previous jobs end?

5. Question: Have you ever been convicted of a crime?
Follow-up: Would you agree to submit to a background check?

6. Question: Would you agree to a trial period before we make a decision for full-time employment?
Follow-up: Are you willing to work the same schedule during your trial period as you would if we brought you on full time? You would be compensated accordingly.

7. Question: Would you be willing to review a nanny agreement with us?

Follow-up: Would you sign the agreement once you have reviewed it? (Keep one copy and return the other copy to us.)

8. Question: Would you like to take a tour of our home?

Follow-up: Do you think our setup is appropriate for our child's needs?

Chapter Two Hours, Travel, Compensation: Crafting the Deal

9. Question: Would you be willing to share a full-time schedule with our family and our friend's family?

Follow-up: Could each family give you set days and hours?

10. Question: Would you be willing to work for us even though we also employ another nanny?

Follow-up: Do you have any hesitations about our "rotating nanny" arrangement?

11. Question: Would you be able to work nontraditional hours?

Follow-up: How many nontraditional hours per week can you work?

12. Question: Are you flexible to work additional hours outside our normal schedule?

Follow-up: How late can you stay at night?

13. Question: Would you be willing to stay overnight at our home when needed?

Follow-up: Is there anything special we can do to make your overnight stay with us more comfortable?

14. Question: Would you like to travel with us?

Follow-up: Will you pack for our child?

15. Question: What are your expectations in terms of pay?
Follow-up: What amount of money have you received in the past from other families?

16. Question: Are you interested in working in our home on a part-time basis?
Follow-up: Are you comfortable with our house rules?

Chapter Three Punctuality, Transportation, Vacations: Clear Expectations

17. Question: Are you a punctual person?
Follow-up: Can you please contact us if you are running late or unable to work?

18. Question: Do you feel comfortable transporting our child, and can you do so safely?
Follow-up: Will you respect our geographic boundaries when transporting our child?

19. Question: Would you provide us with a list of vacation days in advance?
Follow-up: Can you please let us know in advance about any special days you need to arrive late or leave early?

Chapter Four Motivation, Desire, Character: Nanny Management

20. Question: What do you consider to be the ideal priorities for a nanny?
Follow-up: Why would you consider yourself an ideal nanny?

21. Question: What words can be used to describe you?
Follow-up: What are some of your shortcomings?

22. Question: Are you nurturing?
Follow-up: Provide an example of a situation when you felt you nurtured a child.

23. Question: Do you believe you have good judgment?
Follow-up: Please provide an example of how you used good judgment while taking care of a child.

24. Question: Are you a neat person?
Follow-up: Will you either wash my child's hands or make sure my child washes his or her own hands every time he or she comes in from outside the home as well as before all meals?

25. Question: What are your extracurricular activities?
Follow-up: What are some of your hobbies?

26. Question: Are you a festive person?
Follow-up: How would you help a child get into the celebratory spirit?

27. Question: Are you used to caring for children who are extremely active?
Follow-up: Can you deal with a child who may have to be carried or pushed in a stroller?

28. Question: Are you comfortable working for a family who follows certain religious practices?
Follow-up: Would you help drop off our child at religion classes?

Chapter Five House Rules, Daily Routine, Chores, Grooming:
Structuring the Job
29. Question: Will you abide by our house rules?
Follow-up: Do you have issues with any of these rules?

30. Question: Do you have any dietary restrictions or allergies that we should be aware of when you are in our house?
Follow-up: What do you like to eat or drink when taking care of a child?

31. Question: How do you feel about establishing and following daily eating and sleeping routines for the child?
Follow-up: Are you comfortable keeping track of daily activities in a logbook?

32. Question: Do you feel that you have good time-management skills?
Follow-up: Will you be able to keep to my child's schedule?

33. Question: Will you prepare our child's bottles or food?
Follow-up: Are you comfortable cooking, steaming, or pureeing food for our child?

34. Question: Do you feed children inside or outside the home?
Follow-up: Will you abide by our house rules regarding location of the child's meals?

35. Question: Will you make sure the child wears either a bib or appropriate clothing at mealtime?
Follow-up: Will you wash or soak any clothing that the child gets dirty, soiled, or stained under your watch?

36. Question: Would you be willing to do certain household chores when the child is napping or at classes?
Follow-up: What types of chores have other families had you do in the past?

37. Question: Can you clean up food and utensils after meals, clean and sterilize bottles, and tidy up all toys or books at the end of your day?
Follow-up: Would you mind doing the child's laundry on a weekly basis?

38. Question: Are you an organized person?
Follow-up: Would you be willing to help organize our child's schedule, belongings, and supplies?

39. Question: Do you know how to keep children looking neat and well groomed?
Follow-up: Is there anything you do not like to do when it comes to maintenance tasks?

Chapter Six Typical Day: Modeling Your Nanny's Day
40. Question: What do you envision your typical day would be like with my child?
Follow-up: Would you mind incorporating some of my ideas with your ideas so we can work to achieve an ideal day?

41. Question: How do you think a child should be dressed to go outside in warm weather? How about cold weather?
Follow-up: Will you follow a checklist for dressing our child for the outdoors?

42. Question: How do you feel about taking the child on playdates (both indoors and outdoors)?
Follow-up: Do you know other nannies or families in the area?

43. Question: Are you a creative person?
Follow-up: Will you engage my child in creative projects?

44. Question: Would you be willing to take my child to classes that I schedule and pay for?
Follow-up: Will you try to make sure my child is well prepared for the classes?

45. Question: Would you feel comfortable taking my child to a doctor's appointment?
Follow-up: Can you ask the doctor any questions I have and communicate the answers back to me?

46. Question: Would you make sure my child does homework in a quiet place?
Follow-up: Would you be able to supervise my child with homework?

47. Question: Have you ever taken care of a child with developmental issues or special needs?
Follow-up: Would you feel comfortable taking my child to therapy or special classes as well as doing daily exercises recommended by the experts with the child?

48. Question: Do you have experience taking care of older children?
Follow-up: Are you comfortable with taking older children to school and various activities in addition to supervising them in our home?

49. Question: Will you monitor our older child's interactions with peers?
Follow-up: Will you give us feedback on anything that seems interesting, suspicious or unsettling about our child or his or her classmates?

Chapter Seven Safety and Pets: An Extra Level of Protection
50. Question: Do you have any formal training or certifications in childcare?
Follow-up: Please provide an example of an emergency situation and how you handled it.

51. Question: Will you make sure my child is supervised by you at all times?
Follow-up: Will you always be near my child when he or she uses technology?

52. Question: Have your prior families allowed you to bring visitors to their homes?
Follow-up: Who have you brought into their homes?

53. Question: Will you contact me immediately if my child is badly hurt/ injured?
Follow-up: Will you inform me of any accidents that happen involving my child when I am not at home?

54. Question: Do you have pets of your own?
Follow-up: Are you comfortable around pets? Please let us know which household animals you are not comfortable with.

55. Question: How do you feel about children petting animals that do not belong to them?
Follow-up: Will you make sure the child is protected around all animals?

Chapter Eight Situational Questions: 360 Degrees of Insight
56. Question: What position should an infant be in when sleeping in a crib?
Follow-up: Will you keep unnecessary objects out of the baby's crib?

57. Question: What temperature do you believe a baby's room should be at?
Follow-up: Would you please help us maintain a certain temperature in the baby's room?

58. Question: Have you ever experienced a time when a child was crying for an extended period?
Follow-up: How did you handle the crying child?

59. Question: What are your techniques for disciplining a child?
Follow-up: How do you feel about spanking?

60. Question: Have you ever experienced a time when a child had a temper tantrum?
Follow-up: How do you handle an irritable child?

61. Question: Have you ever helped potty train a child?
Follow-up: What successful potty-training techniques have you used for small children?

Chapter Nine Final Question: Final Answer
62. Question: Do you have any questions for us?
Follow-up: Are you interested in working for our family?